D1178983

THE TRAM BOOK

PAUL COLLINS

IAN ALLAN
Publishing

First published 1995

ISBN 0 7110 2268 2

© Paul Collins 1995

Published by Ian Allan Publishing

an imprint of Ian Allan Ltd, Terminal House, Station Approach, Shepperton, Surrey TW17 8AS.
Printed by Ian Allan Printing Ltd, Coombelands House, Coombelands Lane, Addlestone, Surrey KT15 1HY.

Previous page: Leading off the celebrations at the opening of Perth Corporation Tramways on 1 November 1905 was car No 1, seen here at Scone. One of a batch of nine cars, the garlands and drapery seen festooned around the top deck would have set off the tram's lake and cream livery. Never a large system, Perth's fleet grew to just 12 cars, the last of which ran on 19 January 1929. *The late Michael Waller/Peter Waller*

This page: Outside Liverpool Lime Street station on a glorious summer's day in the mid-1920s: Liverpool had the epitome of a big city tramway system — abundant numbers of trams serving a great number of routes, and, within the city centre, broad streets relatively free from other traffic. There is a wealth of detail in this photograph. As tramcars Nos 303 and 122 pass the North Western Hotel, Charlot's Revue is playing at the Empire, and Mr Punch is well into his baby-sitting routine, much to the delight of the crowds in the foreground. *IAL*

CONTENTS

INTRODUCTION
PAGE 4

CHAPTER 1
BEAMS, TRAIN AND CLAUSES —
THE UK'S FIRST TRAMWAY ERA
PAGE 5

CHAPTER 2
HORSE TRAMS
PAGE 9

CHAPTER 3
STEAM, CABLE & OTHER
MECHANICAL TRAMS
PAGE 19

CHAPTER 4
EARLY ELECTRIC TRAMS
& TRAMWAY CONSTRUCTION
PAGE 27

CHAPTER 5
DECORATED TRAMS —
OVERTURE AND
BEGINNERS PLEASE
PAGE 43

CHAPTER 6
ELECTRIC TRAMS TO 1919
PAGE 44

CHAPTER 7
A BIT ON THE SIDE -
TRAMWAY ADVERTISING
PAGE 51

CHAPTER 8
ELECTRIC TRAMS TO 1929
PAGE 53

CHAPTER 9
KEEPING THINGS GOING —
TRAMWAY MAINTENANCE
PAGE 59

CHAPTER 10
ELECTRIC TRAMS TO 1939
PAGE 73

CHAPTER 11
DOING THEIR BIT —
TRAMS AT WAR
PAGE 87

CHAPTER 12
DECORATED TRAMS -
FINALE AND EXIT
PAGE 89

CHAPTER 13
ELECTRIC TRAMS FROM 1945
PAGE 91

CHAPTER 14
TRAMWAY ARCHAEOLOGY
PAGE 107

INTRODUCTION

I can trace my interest in trams back to a very specific point in time. I am child of the television age and one of my favourite programmes was *Blue Peter* (yes, I do have a badge). Watching that essential programme one day, it must have been around 1966 or 1967, they had a feature on trams and showed some film footage of London trams on the Embankment. The reason for the programme featuring trams on that show is forgotten, but its impact upon me is not — I was hooked. What were these bizarre looking things? Where are there any now? — I had to know. I despatched my Father off to our local library and he returned with two books; both were published by Ian Allan and both written by Jim Joyce.

Well, the world turns and here I am, ostensibly grown-up, but still just as interested in trams, and, moreover, writing a tram book for Ian Allan. What will a child of the future, who occasions upon trams over the information superhighway, make of them? Will this book be something they turn to just as I did almost 30 years ago? The responsibility is awesome.

This book owes its existence to a number of people, all of whom I hope I have remembered: John F. Andrews, Nicola Bexon, the staff at Glamorgan Record Office, Mellanie Hartland, Richard Morgan, the staff of the Library at the National Tramway Museum, and Ron Thomas. In addition I would like to pay especial thanks to two people. Firstly to Glyn Wilton, of the Library at the National Tramway Museum, for his thorough knowledge of the amazing collection held there, and for his skills in printing up photographs from it. Secondly I would like to pay special thanks to Peter Waller, whose idea the book was, for his patience and support throughout this project, and for allowing me to use photographs taken and collected by his late father, Michael Waller.

Paul Collins MSc, MSocSc (Ind Arch), PhD
Wollaston, Stourbridge
July, 1995

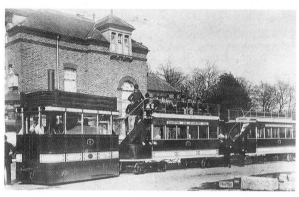

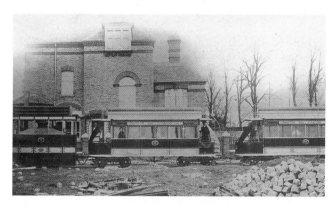

Top:
The Birkdale & Southport Tramways Co Ltd began operating services in 1881. There were two routes, both working from London Square, one to Birkdale, the other to Kew Gardens. Here car No 4 is seen on the Birkdale route. Above the driver's head is the legend: 'SEATS 18 INSIDE, 22 OUTSIDE & 5 ON PLATFORM', but this capacity is hardly strained to its maximum as just one solitary passenger can be seen, sitting on the upper deck's garden-seat-style seating. *IAL*

Middle:
The North London Tramways Co began steam operation along their Stamford Hill-Ponders End route in 1885. It used 15 Merryweather locomotives hauling trailers, often in pairs, as shown. The line had been built in 1881 for single-deck, single-horse trams and was not relaid for use by these much heavier vehicles. This caused track problems, and other mechanical failures were frequent. This view shows locomotive No 3 posed with trailer cars Nos 8 and 2 outside the company's offices. *IAL*

Bottom:
This view shows locomotive No 1 with trailers Nos 11 and 12 again outside the company's offices. Judging by the piles of setts and sections of rail in the yard, track problems were already showing up. *IAL*

BEAMS, TRAIN AND CLAUSES –
THE UK'S FIRST TRAMWAY ERA

With the opening of the Manchester Metrolink and Sheffield Supertram schemes the UK has embarked upon its second tramway era. This book is about trams: horse, steam, cable, other mechanical and mainly, electric trams. It is an attempt to portray through photographs the development and decline of what must now be thought of as the UK's first tramway era.

The word 'tram' comes from a Scandinavian word meaning a beam or baulk of wood. An archaic expression, it was formerly used in this context in the North of England and Scotland. Its connection with transport comes through the use of beams or baulks of timber to act as a guide for wagons in mining and other industrial settings. The guided ways these timbers produced were referred to as 'tramways'.

Apart from such applications the first public tramway was the 9¹/₂-mile Surrey Iron Railway, incorporated by an Act of Parliament on 21 May 1801. This ran from the Thames at Wandsworth to Croydon and opened on 26 July 1803. Solely used for the movement of freight, the line was not a commercial success and it closed on 31 August 1846. Other freight tramways followed the Surrey Iron Railway's example: a 16-mile line opening in Carmarthen in 1804 and the 11-mile Sirhowy Tramroad which came into use in 1805.

But none of these lines carried fare-paying passengers or ran to any kind of published timetable. The first line in the UK, indeed the world, to fulfil these conditions was also in Wales: The Oystermouth Railway, running between Swansea and the Mumbles. It was authorised by an Act of Parliament on 29 June 1804 and freight services began along the line in April 1806. Early in the following year Benjamin French, one of the line's promoters, proposed that he: '*run a waggon or waggons on the Tramroad for one year from the 25th March next, for the conveyance of passengers*'. This was agreed and from 25 March 1807 the Oystermouth Railway became the world's first fare-paying, passenger carrying railway or tramway. French's vehicle was said to have been adapted from one of the line's mineral wagons, although the only known illustration of it, drawn by a 12-year-old girl staying in Swansea in 1819, depicts something more akin to a stagecoach. Pulled by a single horse, the vehicle does have one undeniably tram-like feature — a driving position at either end.

As with more recent innovations, having proven the principle the UK let the development of tramways pass to others, notably the Americans, who saw 'street railways' as

Below:
An artist's impression of Train's Bayswater line taken from a memorial he published and presented to the President of the Board of Trade in 1860. Often presented as an illustration of the line in use, this is pure invention. Double-deck tramcars were not used on the line when it was in operation the following year. *Author's Collection*

an efficient way of moving people around in their developing towns and cities. Thus Baltimore, Ohio, opened America's first street railway in 1828, followed, in 1832, by New York. There the New York & Harlaem (sic) Rail Road, incorporated 25 April 1831, opened a passenger service on 14 November 1832. But this hardly precipitated a spate of openings in other cities, and the only other line to open in the 1830s or the 1840s was the four-mile New Orleans & Carrolton Rail Road, on 26 September 1835. Sixteen years then passed before New York's second line, along Sixth Avenue, opened in 1851, and another five years went by before Boston opened its first street railway. Thereafter more and more cities followed suit. A line opened in Philadelphia in 1857, and by April 1859 there were street railways in Baltimore, Cincinnati, Pittsburgh and Chicago.

In mainland Europe there was little interest in tramways and Paris was the only city to open one, a kind of guided horse-bus line, in 1853. Therefore the Continent presented a golden opportunity for the right person to promote the use of tramways. That 'right person', at least in his own opinion, was an American with a most unfortunate surname given what was to become his place in history: George F. Train. Born in Boston in 1829, Train had amassed a considerable fortune by the age of 30 through running clipper ships. He had encountered street railways in Philadelphia in the late 1850s and immediately recognised both their potential and that of Europe as an otherwise unexplored market for their employment. In those days the UK, especially Liverpool, was the gateway to Europe, the port at which the transatlantic ships docked. And so it was, early in 1860, that George F. Train arrived in Liverpool and, in February that year, began to entreat the authorities there to allow him to lay down a demonstration line for his street railways.

Liverpool already had a tramway of sorts: a line similar to the Paris example, operated by William J. Curtis along the Mersey Docks & Harbour Board's rails from 1858. In the face of Train's requests the Liverpool authorities prevaricated and in frustration he turned to those in neighbouring Birkenhead. Only a river's width away, Birkenhead was in a different county to Liverpool — Cheshire — and was a town in which there was little love lost between its inhabitants and those 'across the water'. Train made approaches to the Birkenhead authorities in March 1860 and these were met with an altogether more favourable response. On 7 May 1860 he registered the Birkenhead Street Railway Co Ltd and three months later, on 30 August 1860, he opened a 1¼-mile horse tramway line between Woodside Ferry and Birkenhead Park. The line was successful and, overcoming a slight hiccup in 1864, expanded and developed.

Still the Liverpool authorities hummed and hawed, but Train had lost interest as a result of their indecisiveness. London was his goal: prove yourself in London, and Europe would be opened up to you, he believed. And so Train began to petition the President of the Board of Trade with memorials to the excellence of his street railway system. Let him lay down demonstration lines somewhere in the capital

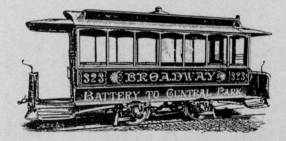

John Stephenson Company,
LIMITED.

47 EAST 27TH STREET,

NEW YORK.

Tram · Car · Builders,

INVITE THE ATTENTION OF

PROMOTERS OF ELECTRIC RAILWAY ENTERPRISES

TO THEIR

Superior Facilities

For the Construction of

Tramway Cars,

AND FOR THEIR ADAPTATION TO THE

VARIOUS SCHEMES OF

ELECTRIC PROPULSION.

Left:
An American advertisement for John Stephenson Co Ltd, New York, the firm who supplied many of the first horse trams to British operators. *Author's Collection*

Opposite above:
The Oystermouth Railway, which was more descriptively known as the Swansea & Mumbles Railway in its later years, was the first passenger-carrying railway or tramway in the world. This service began on or about Lady Day (25 March) 1807 and ran, sporadically, until some time in 1827 when passenger services along the line were abandoned through competition from horse-buses working along a newly completed turnpike. Goods services continued for some time but the whole line was relaid in the late 1850s and passenger services were reintroduced on 10 November 1860 using vehicles like the one shown. Photographed in 1865, this odd mixture of a railway carriage and a stagecoach appears rather more than just one poor horse could manage by itself. *Ian Allan Library (IAL)*

Opposite below:
A Belfast City Tramways car on the Ligoniel route pauses to be photographed. Horse trams were introduced into the city by the Belfast Street Tramways Co Ltd on 28 August 1872. The track was laid to the standard gauge and the company used only single-deck cars for its first six years of operation. The opening of additional routes and the extension of others led to a demand for greater capacity on the trams and so double-decked cars, like the one seen here, were introduced in 1878. The addition of a pair of 'trace' or 'cock' horses to the single pair usually employed indicates that the car had just tackled or was about to tackle a hilly section of the route. *National Tramway Museum Collection*

and everyone would see the truth behind what he way saying. More prevarication followed, and concerted opposition from the London General Omnibus Co saw out 1860. By January 1861 Train had decided to lay his line down along the Bayswater Road, and that month he registered the Marble Arch Street Rail Co Ltd. Agreement, rather than Parliamentary approval, was secured for the line that ran from Porchester Terrace to Edgware Road — a distance of just under a mile — and opened on 23 March 1861.

A public relations triumph, Train's tramway was the talk of London, and on 15 April 1861 he opened a second line along Victoria Street. An indication of the haste in which this was done comes from the fact that the company that operated the line — the Westminster Street Rail Co Ltd — was not registered until 22 April 1861. Four months later, on 15 August 1861, Train's third and final London demonstration line opened, from Westminster Bridge to Kennington Gate, this being operated by the Surrey Side Street Rail Co Ltd. (This company was registered on 29 May 1861.) In the space of five months Train had three demonstration lines working in London. They were a hit with the public but less popular with the competition and other road users. Train's tramways used 'step rails', which bore a flange that stood proud of the roadway, and were single lines laid on one side of the road, so that when working in one direction his vehicles were moving against the prevailing flow of traffic. Complaints

mounted, notably from the not disinterested London General Omnibus Co, and in September 1861 the Bayswater line closed. Similar disputes forced the closure of the Victoria Street line on 6 March 1862 and the Westminster Bridge one on 21 June 1862, the latter whilst workers were tearing up the lines.

Bloodied but unbowed, Train had already turned his attention northwards again. Approaches were made to various towns and cities. One example is Birmingham

where, on 7 August 1860, he obtained permission to lay a line from New Street to the Ivy Bush Inn on the Hagley Road but, as one contemporary observer recorded, Train: '*after yarning us well … his glib tongue failed in procuring the needful capital (and) his scheme was a thorough failure*'.

Greater success was enjoyed elsewhere, and on 1 January 1862 one of Train's companies began to operate a line between Bank Top and the Market Place in Darlington, and on 13 January that year the Staffordshire Potteries Street Railway Co Ltd (registered 22 November 1861) opened a line between Foundry Street, Hanley and Burslem Town Hall. This would be the extent of George F. Train's street railways in the UK. With his London lines closed and lifted, and no nearer his goal of Europe, Train returned to the USA in 1862, where, later, he would build the Union Pacific Railroad.

What was Train's legacy to the UK? His London lines were temporary; the most one survived was 11 months, and his Darlington line closed on 31 December 1864. But the Birkenhead line thrived and the Potteries line, relaid with grooved rail in 1864, became part of the North Staffordshire Tramways system in 1880. Outside these tangible achievements, Train demonstrated the tram's potential, an example others would follow.

Another variant on the theme of a guided horse-bus line opened between Pendleton, Peel Park and Market Street, Salford in August 1860, running until around 1866. Tramways were also opened on the Isle of Wight (29 August 1864) and at Portsmouth (15 May 1865), and interest in the promotion of lines increased generally by the end of the 1860s, so much so that Parliament decided to produce a general Tramways Act to reduce the amount of Parliamentary time the processing of individual tramways' acts was taking.

The Tramways Act became law on 9 August 1870. It was designed to protect those local authorities through which tramway schemes were promoted. To encourage local authority involvement in tramway operation the Act contained a number of clauses, four of which were to become notorious in the history of UK tramways:

- Local authorities were given the power of absolute veto upon any proposed tramway construction in their streets. No appeal was allowed against these decisions;
- Local authorities were given a right of compulsory purchase of tramways in their area after 21 years at 'old iron prices';

- Tramway operators were required to pave and repair the roadway in between their track(s) and for a distance of 18 inches outside of this;
- The land occupied by tram tracks was to be assessed at its full value for rating purposes.

Tramway schemes seeking approval under the Tramways Act could be granted a Provisional Order to enable them to proceed, but each had to be confirmed by the passing of a separate Parliamentary Act. The effects of this Act were far-reaching:

- In London the veto was exercised to great effect by the City Corporation who forbade the laying of lines in and through the heart of the city, thereby excluding efficient cross-city tram links;
- By the 1890s, when many tramways were facing the prospect of compulsory purchase by local authorities, reinvestment in new track, rolling stock, or innovations such as electrification, were deferred;
- On roads with double lines of standard gauge track, tramway operators were effectively paving the entire road surface;
- Taxing land occupied by tram tracks was bad enough, but the extra three feet of road width required to be paved was assessed at its full rateable value too.

The Tramways Act was revised in 1880, but the punishing clauses mentioned above remained.

Tramway promoters fared better under terms of the Light Railways Act, 1896, although this had been passed to aid railway rather than tramway construction. The Act permitted:

- Companies to hold land and acquire it by compulsory purchase;
- Lines to be laid nearer to kerbs than permitted by the Tramways Act, 1870;
- Five years to complete a scheme, compared to the two years permitted by the Tramways Act, 1870;
- Assessment of land occupied by tracks at one fourth of its net annual value for rating purposes.

Tramway schemes seeking approval under the Light Railways Act also obtained a Provisional Order to enable them to proceed, but this did not have to be confirmed by a separate Parliamentary Act.

This is the history and background against which much of the UK's first tramway era developed.

Above:
In Aberdeen the District Tramways Co opened its first route on 31 August 1874. The cars serving each route were painted in their own distinctive livery and were numbered in separate sequences for each route. Aberdeen Corporation took over the running of the trams on 25 August 1898, and the fleet was repainted with the city crest. Here, shortly after the Corporation take-over, car No 9 is seen at Queen's Cross on the circular route. *National Tramway Museum Collection*

2

HORSE TRAMS

Much of the interest and general enthusiasm that exists for trams nowadays is directed towards electric trams. This is understandable for they are the closest to living memory and, in modern parlance, 'sexier'. As a result, the older manifestations of the tram, most notably the steam and horse tram, tend to be overlooked or regarded as mere curiosities. Less technical they may have been, although that distinction is hardly true of the steam tram, but without the tram's earlier forms the later ones would not have existed. Horse trams in particular 'proved the point' with regard to the principle of the street tramway, and in many British towns and cities they gave good service as a mass 'people mover' during two or three decades leading up to the turn of the 20th century.

The initial capital outlay incurred in building a tramway was considerable, partly due to the requirements of the 1870 Tramways Act. Some illustrative examples are:

- Bristol Tramways Co, which spent £14,000 on building a 1³/₄-mile line in 1874/75;
- Cambridge Street Tramways Co, which raised a working capital of £20,000 in £10 shares to install a 2²/₃-mile tramway at a cost of £3,167 per mile in 1879/80;
- St Helens District Tramways Co, which tried to raise an authorised capital of £70,000 for just over 11 miles of line, built at £3,700 per mile in 1880-82.

Due to the advantages of railed transport, not the least of which is the greatly reduced friction between a metal wheel and a metal track, a horse could pull a much larger vehicle, and hence more passengers, on a tramway than it could on the road. As a result, horse trams could be built much larger

Right and below:
The Leicester Tramway Co Ltd's horse tram No 37 has the High Street pretty much to itself as it plies its way towards the Clock Tower. It must have been some kind of occasion as Union Flags and other flags are flying further down the street. Leicester's first horse trams ran from the Clock Tower to Belgrave on 24 December 1874, with additional routes to Humberstone Road and Shrubbery (London Road) opening on 23 March and 14 August 1875. The cars were painted in an unusual colour mix of grey and biscuit. Further routes opened in 1878 and the company's lines were not sold to the Corporation until 31 December 1902. Work to electrify and expand the tramway system then began; Leicester's last horse tram, car No 22, ran on 17 May 1904, and car No 9 is seen during the Corporation's relatively brief period as a horse tram operator.
National Tramway Museum Collection (both)

and roomier than contemporary horse omnibuses, and the ride on the tramway was also much smoother than that afforded by the rutted and pitted roads their more peripatetic cousins plied along, especially when the permanent way was new. A typical horse omnibus could seat between 12-15 persons whilst a horse tram could seat 25-40. Horse trams had brakes too, and so they were not stopped solely by the act of pulling up the horses. Each of these advantages helped to make horse trams more popular, and their operation more profitable, than omnibuses or carriages.

The coming of the railways had effectively killed off the demand for long distance stagecoaches. Many former stagecoach operators turned to short-haul work, ferrying railway passengers into town centres from often remote stations. Some coach operators subsequently developed local omnibus routes, most of which began or terminated outside railway stations, and in doing so they inherited and preserved many of the practices and terminology from the carriage and stagecoach trade, which, in turn, horse tramway operators adopted. Thus, for example, stabling practice was well established, and the extra horses attached to trams when climbing hills were still called 'cock' or 'trace' horses, as they had been in the stagecoach era.

A good deal of the development of the basic design of the British tramcar took place with horse trams, and it was essentially their final form that was electrified in the 1890s. The earliest horse trams were built to American patterns developed by companies such as the J. G. Brill Co, Philadelphia, the Brownell & Wight Car Co, St Louis, the Lewis & Fowler Manufacturing Co, Brooklyn, New York, and John Stephenson Co Ltd, New York; the latter's cars being particularly favoured by British tramway companies. Tramcar manufacture was also established in the UK, the earliest being by George Starbuck, who had been George F. Train's manager in Birkenhead. Starbuck's secretary, George F. Milnes, later took over his business and founded a large tramcar works at Hadley, near Wellington in Shropshire. Established railway carriage and wagon

manufacturers also started to make tramcars, as did some of the larger omnibus proprietors, such as Solomon Andrews in Cardiff.

Single-decked horse trams weighed around 30cwt, seated between 14 and 18, and required one horse to draw them; double-deckers weighed $2\frac{1}{2}$ tons and required a pair of horses; they seated 20 or so downstairs and around 24 on the top deck. Upper-deck seating was of the 'knifeboard' kind, that is a pair of longitudinal seats placed back-to-back along the centre-line of the roof. Bright colours were used to decorate the trams, often a different one for each route, and the cars were sometimes given names evoking speed or modernity, just as stagecoaches had been a generation or two earlier. The interiors of the cars were upholstered and the windows had curtains, whilst the upper decks were Spartan in comparison, having just polished wooden seats and a safety rail. At night, oil lamps illuminated the lower saloon, giving off an unpleasant smell. The horses were harnessed to a draw bar that was coupled to the car by a pin, the removal of which made changing horses an easy matter.

Opposite above:
A fine example of a two-horse tramcar built by Solomon Andrews & Sons at their workshops in Oxford Street, Cardiff, in 1881. The builders also used the car on the Cardiff District & Penarth Harbour Tramway Co's $2\frac{1}{2}$-mile line between Splotlands and Grangetown in Cardiff. This opened on 29 November 1881 and operated until the sale of Solomon Andrews' interest in the Cardiff District & Penarth Harbour Tramway Co on 7 May 1888.
S. Andrews & Son Collection

Opposite centre and below:
Lincoln's first tramway was a 3ft 6in gauge line to Bracebridge that opened in 1882. One-horse single-deck cars were used on the line, vehicles that unusually, eschewed any declaration of their ownership in favour of advertisements. In the city one car proclaims the virtues of Mr Cadbury's Cocoa and Mr White's Speciality Cakes, whilst at Bracebridge terminus, strike-a-light if the crew of car No 5 aren't testimony to the excellence of Bryant & May's matches.
National Tramway Museum Collection (both)

Right:
Two views of Paisley District Tramways Co's cars at or near to the end of their operation. The company began as the Paisley Tramways Co Ltd and opened a one mile four furlongs and 95 chains-long 4ft 7¾in gauge line on 30 December 1885. The single-deck car is No 48, photographed outside the company's stables and depot at Incle Street in late 1903. What appears to be a top-deck seat is just an advertising board. To the right of the double-deck car a traction pole can be seen, showing that installation of the overhead for the replacement electric trams was well in hand. The British Electric Traction Co first expressed an interest in acquiring the horse tramway in 1897, but Glasgow Corporation also showed an interest. An impasse followed and Paisley Council resolved this by establishing its own company, the Paisley District Tramways Co, to operate the tramway. The latter assumed the assets of the former company on 3 January 1903, but only operated horse trams until 21 November that year, an electric tramway service beginning on 13 June 1904.
National Tramway Museum Collection (both)

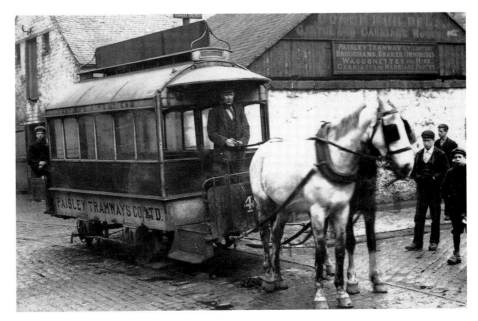

Above:
Not all horse tramways were lucrative. The Pontypridd & Rhondda Valley Tramway Co Ltd was incorporated in 1885 and opened a three-mile line between Pontypridd and Porth on 26 March 1888, but it never paid. Here a double-deck car waits at Porth terminus, by the Commercial Hotel, where the photographer seems to be the object of much curiosity. Responding to interest from the British Electric Traction Co, the company was purchased on 28 September 1898 and closed.
C. Batson

Opposite above:
In 1893, when a number of horse tramways were run down or already closed, the great omnibus manufacturer and proprietor Solomon Andrews acquired the first portion of what was to become an estate at Pwllheli in North Wales. Intent upon developing the area, known as West End, as a holiday resort, he set about building a promenade,

houses and the West End Hotel. To carry building stone the 2½ miles from a quarry at Carreg-y-defaid, Andrews had a 3ft 6in gauge tramway laid down. Here part of the line can be seen running past some of the promenade houses Solomon Andrews built. *S. Andrews & Son Collection*

Opposite below:
A behind-the-scenes look in the Hazel Grove depot of the Stockport & Hazel Grove Tramway Co Ltd. This was situated at the rear of the Crown Inn on Wellington Road South, Great Moor. The company had begun a half-hourly service between St Peter's Square and the Rising Sun Inn, Hazel Grove, on Good Friday 4 April 1890. Originally, garden seat-style double-deckers of the kind seen on the right were used, but in 1891 single-deckers like the one seen on the left were also introduced. After lengthy negotiations Stockport Corporation bought the tramway company for £24,000 on 24 October 1904, auctioning its assets at the Crown Inn on 11-12 July 1905. *National Tramway Museum Collection*

Gradually, improvements were made to horse tram design. One innovation was the Eades Patent Reversible mechanism that enabled the tramcar's body to be turned around at termini, obviating both the need to change the horses around and for the car to have stairs at both ends. But, despite its ingenuity, the Eades design was only taken up extensively by tramway operators in Chester, Liverpool, Manchester, Nottingham, plus those in a few other places. Another development was the adoption of transverse rather than longitudinal seating for the top deck, from around 1886. Two rows of seats with reversible backs were laid out along a central gangway — the adoption of the classic tramcar seating form — known as the 'garden seat' arrangement. The cars also increased in size and, in the 1890s, designs with larger windows began to appear.

And what of the motive power for these tramcars? Horse tram operators reckoned that an average of 10 horses was required for each car in service. This was based upon the assumption that over a 15hr working day each horse or pair of horses would only haul a tram for about three hours or so. As a result, even a modest fleet of around 20 tramcars required, potentially, 200 horses to operate it. Moreover, each horse had to be stabled in its own stall, fed, groomed, shod and generally well looked after, with its — eh-hem —

by-products disposed of! Horses were put to tram or omnibus work at around five years, such an animal costing anything between £25 and £35. A tramway operator could expect about four years of good work from each horse, which would then be sold on for other work, fetching around £5, or as a carcass for £1 to £1 10s.

A good illustration of the operation of a horse tramway can be found in the Statement of Accounts for the Half-Year ending 30 June 1892 of the Leicester Tramways Co Ltd. During this period the company had:

- Gross Receipts   £17,001 1s 4d
- Gross Expenditure   £14,549 11s 2d
- Gross Profit   £2,573 5s 2d

causing the Chairman to comment that: *'The business of the Company has been of a satisfactory character, and continues to show progress. Additional stabling has been erected at Belgrave and the number of Horses increased; three new Omnibuses have been purchased and one new Car has been built by the Company at their own works, and two others are in the course of construction. A large outlay has been made on renewal of the Permanent Way, and still further heavy expenditure in this department will be necessary.'*

ABSTRACTS.

ABSTRACT "A."—HORSE RENEWAL ACCOUNT.

	£ s. d.	£ s. d.
Horse Renewal Account as per last half-year's Balance Sheet		2,370 1 5
Add Horses Sold during half-year (19)	196 19 0	
„ Amount charged to Capital Account (No. 1), for 24 additional Horses purchased during half-year	1,008 0 0	
		1,204 19 0
		3,575 0 5
Less Horses purchased during half-year (43)		1,786 17 6
Horse Renewal Account, 30th June, 1892		£1,788 2 11

ABSTRACT "B."—HORSING EXPENSES.

	£ s. d.
Forage Account (as per Abstract "E")	4,740 19 6
Granary Wages	131 7 1
Horsekeepers' Wages	1,103 10 7
Shoeing	316 19 11
Horse Medicine and Veterinary Services	55 13 11
Rent, Rates, and Taxes—Stables and Granary	117 3 1
Gas, Water, and Coal	123 18 1
Stable Repairs	94 10 1
Utensils and Sundries	58 8 6
Stoker's Wages, Boiler and Engine Repairs	28 11 6
	6,771 2 3
Less Manure	137 12 8
	£6,633 9 7

ABSTRACT "C."—TRAFFIC EXPENSES.

	£ s. d.
Drivers and Guards' Wages	3,475 3 9
Traffic Superintendence	186 14 11
Rent, Rates, and Taxes)	78 8 4
Repairs (Car Sheds, Workshops, and Offices)	22 18 3
Gas and Water)	58 8 1
Car Lighting and Oiling	62 19 7
Car Washing	201 17 10
Track Cleaning	28 10 4
Traffic Stationery, Way Bills, &c.	53 9 4
Traffic Office Clerks' Salaries	181 14 0
Repairs to Fare Boxes	2 10 3
Salt and Sand	63 9 7
Licenses and Excise	25 1 0
Compensation	55 13 0
	£4,496 18 3

ABSTRACT "D."—GENERAL EXPENSES.

	£ s. d.
Directors' Fees	250 0 0
Auditors' Fees	21 0 0
Salaries—Manager and Secretary	250 0 0
Law Charges	5 12 8
Insurance	24 3 9
Printing and Stationery	20 19 11
Office, Bank, and General Expenses	72 11 7
	£644 7 11

ABSTRACT "E."—DETAILS OF FORAGE ACCOUNT.

	MAIZE.			OATS.			BEANS.		
	Price per Qr.	Quantity.	Amount.	Price per Qr.	Quantity.	Amount.	Price per Qr.	Quantity.	Amount.
	s. d.	Qrs.	£ s. d.	s. d.	Qrs.	£ s. d.	s. d.	Qrs.	£ s. d.
On hand Jan. 1st, 1892.	34 0	100	170 0 0	23 6	10	11 15 0	40 0	8	16 0 0
Purchased since	25 5	776	986 3 9	22 8¾	947½	1077 6 9	38 1½	381½	727 11 9
	26 4¾	876	1156 3 9	22 9	957½	1089 1 9	38 2	389½	743 11 9
Consumed	26 5¼	851	1124 18 9	22 9	957½	1089 1 9	38 5	364½	700 9 3
On hand June 30, 1892. Taken at Cost Price.	25 0	25	31 5 0	...	...	... ...	34 6	25	43 2 6

	BARLEY.			BRAN.			OATMEAL.		
	Price per Qr.	Quantity.	Amount.	Price per Cwt	Quantity.	Amount.	Price per Cwt.	Quantity.	Amount.
	s. d.	Qrs.	£ s. d.	s. d.	Cwts.	£ s. d.	s. d.	Cwts.	£ s. d.
On hand Jan. 1st, 1892.	...	...	.. ...	6 0	1	0 6 0	17 2	5	4 6 0
Purchased since	30 0	49	73 10 0	5 10½	14	4 2 3	16 0	37½	30 0 0
	30 0	49	73 10 0	5 10½	15	4 8 3	16 1¼	42½	34 6 0
Consumed	30 0	49	73 10 0	5 11½	10	2 19 9	16 1¾	37½	30 6 0
On hand June 30, 1892. Taken at Cost Price.	... ...	...	... ...	5 8½	5	1 8 6	16 0	5	4 0 0

	HAY AND CLOVER.			STRAW.			SAWDUST.			MOSS LITTER.			SUNDRIES.
	Price per Ton.	Quantity.	Amount.	Price per Ton.	Quantity.	Amount.	Price per Sack.	Quantity.	Amount.	Price per Ton.	Quantity.	Amount.	Amount.
	s. d.	Tons.	£ s. d.	s. d.	Tons.	£ s. d.	s. d.	Sacks.	£ s. d.	s. d.	Tons.	£ s. d.	£ s. d.
On hand Jan. 1st, 1892.	80 0	20	80 0 0	...	...	... ...	...	...	... ...	.. ..	...	... ...	14 2 0
Purchased since	80 11½	344	1392 10 8	55 4½	1¾	4 16 11	0 3	2735	34 11 11	28 2¾	75	105 17 2	87 15 4
	80 11	364	1472 10 8	55 4½	1¾	4 16 11	0 3	2735	34 11 11	28 2¾	75	105 17 2	101 17 4
Consumed	80 11	364	1472 10 8	55 4½	1¾	4 16 11	0 3	2735	34 11 11	28 2¾	75	105 17 2	101 17 4
On hand June 30, 1892. Taken at Cost Price.	...	...	... ...	... ...	..	... ...	... ...	...	... ...	... ...	...	... ...	... ...

Total Cost of Forage (including Bedding and Sundries) £4,740 19 6
Average Number of Horses 301
Average Cost per Horse per Week for past Half-year ... ... s. d. 12 1·39
Ditto ditto for Half-year ending 30th June, 1891 ... ... 12 4·90

Decrease of 3·51 per Horse per week.

In the half-year the company operated 40 trams (nine one-horse and 31 two-horse), 29 omnibuses and seven brakes, with 317 horses. During the period they carried 3,817,032 passengers over 376,503 miles, collecting £16,508 2s 10d in fares. The General Manager reported that of the company's horses, three were on sale and four off work from lameness and colds, and that during the half-year 48 horses had been purchased and 19 sold.

Much detail of the company's operation can be gleaned from the various 'Abstracts' (above & left) published with these half-yearly accounts. Five of these are reproduced, covering: Horse Renewal, Horsing Expenses, Traffic Expenses, General Expenses and the Forage Account.

Given George F. Train's attempts to promote tramways in the UK's larger towns and cities, and his similar designs on Europe, it is perhaps surprising to see the places in which tramways were established. For whilst there were successful systems installed in cities such as Belfast, Aberdeen, Leicester, Cardiff and Lincoln, towns such as Southport, Paisley and Stockport also built tramways, as did remoter industrial communities in Wales. And then, just as genuine horse power was giving way to the mechanically-generated kind, a new horse tramway was built to serve a seaside development at Pwllheli in North Wales.

Most of the UK's horse tramways went on to be mechanised, either serving a period worked by steam traction or going on directly to form the basis of an expanded electrified tramway system. There were some exceptions though, most notably the 'Oxbridge' cities of Oxford and Cambridge, whose horse tramways were not electrified and were both closed during the early months of 1914. Horse trams at the seaside seemed to fare better; they had an obvious appeal as a visitor attraction and, as the vehicles became a scarcer part of the everyday scene, they also gained a novelty value. Thus Morecambe held on to its horse trams until the end of the holiday season in 1926, and Pwllheli's line would have continued but for a serious landslide in 1927. In quieter rural areas too, where the pace of life was slower, the horse tram found a niche, and in Fintona, in Eire, one remained in use until 1957. Today only Douglas on the Isle of Man has a working horse tramway. The system, the first part of which opened in August 1876, thrives on tourism and uses a fleet of cars, many of which were built originally a century or more ago.

WEST END TRAMWAYS, PWLLHELI.

2½ MILES ALONG THE "UNRIVALLED SOUTH BEACH."

On and after August 1st, 1896, the above Trams will leave the West End Hotel and Careg-y-defaid as under, weather permitting, until further notice :---

Leaves West End Hotel.		Leaves Carreg-y-Defaid.	
9 0 a.m.	4 0 p.m.	9 20 a.m.	4 20 p.m.
9 40 a.m.	4 2½ p.m.	10 0 a.m.	4 40 p.m.
10 20 a.m.	4 40 p.m.	10 40 a.m.	5 20 p.m.
11 0 a.m.	5 0 p.m.	11 20 a.m.	5 40 p.m.
11 40 a.m.	5 20 p.m.	12 0 n'n.	6 0 p.m.
12 20 p.m.	5 40 p.m.	12 40 p.m.	6 20 p.m.
1 0 p.m.	6 0 p.m.	1 0 p.m.	6 40 p.m.
1 40 p.m.	6 20 p.m.	2 0 p.m.	7 0 p.m.
2 0 p.m.	6 40 p.m.	2 20 p.m.	7 20 p.m.
2 20 p.m.	7 0 p.m.	2 40 p.m.	7 40 p.m.
2 40 p.m.	7 20 p.m.	3 0 p.m.	8 0 p.m.
3 0 p.m.	7 40 p.m.	3 20 p.m.	8 20 p.m.
3 20 p.m.	8 0 p.m.	3 40 p.m.	8 40 p.m.
3 40 p.m.	8 20 p.m.	4 0 p.m.	

Fares: 2d. each way.

- -

Omnibuses, in connection with the above Tramways, will run from West End Hotel to Town and Station, and vice versa.

Fares :-- {West End Hotel to Town, 1d.} and vice versa.
{Town to Station, 1d.}

S. ANDREWS & SON, PROPRIETORS.

Office :--CARDIFF ROAD.

— TO LET, —
For Concerts, &c., West End Assembly Rooms.
Seat, 450. Terms: Apply—T. CUNNINGHAM, Cardiff Road.

Printed by Owen Humphreys, 47, High Street, Pwllheli.

Above:
The West End Tramways at Pwllheli used a variety of rolling stock, including this toast-rack car seen passing the end of the near-completed terraces adjoining the West End Hotel. *S. Andrews & Son Collection*

Left:
Solomon Andrews' tramway also carried passengers, and 'on and after' 1 August 1896 the above service was operated from the West End Hotel to the Town and on to the railway station. *John F. Andrews*

PWLLHELI & LLANBEDROG
TRAMWAYS.
TIME TABLE JULY & AUGUST, 1897.

LEAVE PWLLHELI.	LEAVE LLANBEDROG.
8-15 a.m.	9-0 a.m.
9.45 ,,	10.30 ,,
10.30 ,,	11.15 ,,
11.15 ,,	12.0 noon.
12.0 noon	12.45 p.m.
12.45 p.m.	1.30 ,,
1.30 ,,	2.0 ,,
2.0 ,,	2.30 ,,
2.30 ,,	3.0 ,,
3.0 ,,	3.30 ,,
3.30 ,,	4.0 ,,
4.0 ,,	4.30 ,,
4.30 ,,	5.0 ,,
5.0 ,,	5.30 ,,
5.30 ,,	6.0 ,,
6.0 ,,	6.30 ,,
6.30 ,,	7.15 ,,
7.15 ,,	8.0 ,,
8.0 ,,	8.45 ,,

A WORKMEN'S CAR will leave Pwllheli daily for Llanbedrog at 6-30 a.m., and return therefrom at 5-45 p.m. Fare 2d. each way.

Cars run every 20 Minutes on Fair Days, Bank Holidays, &c.,

FARES :—

Pwllheli to Llanbedrog........4d.	West End Hotel,
,, Carreg y Defaid 3d.	to
Children under 13...............2d.	Pwllheli............................1d.
and vice versa.	

FINE ART GALLERY NOW OPEN.

Visitors should not miss seeing Glynyweddw Mansion, now converted into a Fine Art Gallery, and Ornamental Pleasure Gardens. There is a grand collection of Paintings and Drawings by Turner , David Cox, Prout, P. de Wint, Stanfield, Muller, Copley Fielding, J. B. Pyne, J. Syer, Nasmyth. S. Bough, D. Teneirs, Cooper, Elmore, and other noted Artists. Refreshment Rooms on the Grounds. Entrance opposite Tramway Terminus. Admission, 6d.

Office : Cardiff Road.

S. ANDREWS & SON,
Proprietors.

Printed by Owen Humphreys, Commercial House, Pwllheli.

Left:
In 1897 the Pwllheli tramway was extended to another estate bought by Solomon Andrews at Llanbedrog, and renamed the Pwllheli & Llanbedrog Tramways. The above is one of the first timetables published for the new line.
John F. Andrews

Below:
A tremendous, if not somewhat illusory, impression of speed is conveyed in this 1920s view of an open car on the Pwllheli & Llanbedrog tramway pulling up at West End terminus.
S. Andrews & Son Collection

Top:
Immensely popular with holidaymakers, the Pwllheli & Llanbedrog tramway continued until 1927. By that time its trackbed was in a poor condition. During the line's last summer, an oncoming car is seen being re-railed near the approach to Llanbedrog. *IAL*

Above:
The Pwllheli & Llanbedrog tramway ran until 28 October 1927. On that night heavy seas washed away portions of the line and covered others with sand. The cost of reinstating the line, and of holding back future erosion, was considered too great and it was abandoned. This view shows the approach to Llanbedrog during the last summer of operation. *IAL*

STEAM, CABLE & OTHER MECHANICAL TRAMS

Horse trams may well have proved the point so far as the principle of tramways was concerned but they also proved costly to operate and yielded poor, if any, profits. Fares reflected this, and tramway operators' attempts to recoup profits through high fares had the obvious effect of reducing passenger numbers. What was needed was a less costly, more reliable and efficient means of hauling tramcars. In the last quarter of the 19th century much ingenuity was applied to this quest, sometimes pushing available technology and engineering up to and beyond its limits. Only two serious contenders emerged — steam and cable — but human imagination was allowed free and full rein in coming up with some alternatives.

STEAM TRAMS

If, in theory, all British tramways could have been mechanically-hauled from their respective opening dates, then the means of hauling them would most certainly have been steam traction. The technology that deposited people at railway stations, from where some had the option of taking horse trams to get them nearer to their destinations, was as old as the 19th century. Trevithick, Rastrick, the Stephensons and others had all contributed to the refinement of a technology that had already proven its adaptability — surely running on rails through the streets was just one more logical application? True, although when did logic ever have anything to do with what actually happens?

Those wishing to use steam haulage on tramways came face-to-face with two problems. The first was legal, in that steam tramway operation was deemed to come under the terms of the Locomotives on Highways Act. This legislation had been passed to protect turnpikes from being chewed— and churned-up by steam-powered road vehicles, and had followed on directly from a number of experimental uses of steam carriages and omnibuses during the 1830s and 1840s. Tolls were specified, weights, dimensions and speeds restricted, and the vehicles had to be preceded

by someone carrying a red flag. It didn't seem to matter that steam trams would be running on rails, along a predetermined course and not wearing away the road surface — the law was the law. Indeed, it was this same peculiar piece of legislation — at turns loosely worded and tightly restrictive — that hampered the use of early motor cars, all of which also had to be preceded by someone with a red flag!

The second problem facing potential steam tramway operators, especially those who already ran horse trams, was the extra weight of the locomotives. This often exceeded the limit of existing track, as some came to find out to their cost. Steam trams also caused extra wear on rails, notably on curves.

It might be assumed that the Tramways Act, 1870, being specifically drafted to assist the passage of tramway bills through Parliament and, more generally, to promote the development of tramways, would have included provisions for their mechanical haulage. In fact the Act made a specific assumption that 'animal power' would be used on tramways unless a Special Act of Parliament was obtained to the contrary. Thus the Tramways Act gave some succour to the proponents of mechanical haulage, but few chose to obtain a Special Act and put this to the test.

There had been experiments with steam haulage on tramways in the United States from 1831, when the New York & Harlaem system had tried to use it on their first line. The company tried again in 1837, when two locomotives, called, appropriately enough, *New York* and *Harlaem*, were used on their lines. Steam trams were also used in Philadelphia between 1859 and 1861. In the UK, a self-contained steam tram, with locomotive and passenger

Right:
A steam tram and its crew, showing the general arrangement of the locomotive and trailer car. The driver is standing at the leading or firebox end, in front of the locomotive's vertical boiler. The effectiveness of the protective valance around the bottom of the locomotive is apparent, in screening the wheels and motion . Behind, the continuous 'on-one-level' platform and lower saloon floor of the trailer car can be seen, as can the position of the bogies at the extreme ends of the car. Most of the upper deck has been enclosed. *IAL*

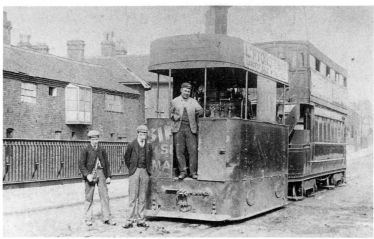

sections in one unit, was tried illegally on the London Tramways Co's line in Vauxhall Bridge Road in the early hours of 26 November 1873, but it could barely produce enough power to move itself, let alone any passengers.

The development of the steam tram locomotive is a subject worthy of its own consideration and outside the scope of the present book; it has also been well covered by others. It represents a near perfect example of the adaptation of a proven technology to fulfil a specific application, all achieved within the space of 10-12 years. Clearly, railway locomotives were unsuitable for use in the streets. They were too large, and hence heavy, for this purpose, and they produced excessive smoke and had exposed and dangerous motions and valve gear. On tramways, the load to be hauled was much less than on a railway, with far less drag, but far tighter curves had to be negotiated. From even these simple observations some of the requirements of a steam tram locomotive become apparent. They needed to be or to have:

- small in size
- light in weight
- reduced smoke emissions
- covered or protected motion
- a short wheelbase, better to negotiate tight curves

Export sales spurred the first developments of the steam tram locomotive. Manning, Wardle & Co of Leeds built some specially adapted locomotives for the 4ft gauge Pernambuco Tramways, Brazil, in 1867. These were essentially 0-4-0 saddle tank locomotives with outside cylinders, condensing equipment and an all-over cab. Other examples include:

- Leonard Todd of Leith who designed a steam tramway locomotive for a tramway in Spain in 1871, the first such locomotive designed specifically for a tramway;
- Merryweather & Sons of Greenwich who patented a tramway locomotive in April 1875;
- John Downes of Birmingham who designed a tramway locomotive that was built for him by Henry Hughes & Co of Loughborough in 1875.

Downes' locomotive was tried in service, with fare-paying passengers, running between Handsworth and West Bromwich on 8 January 1876 — the first such use in the UK.

Technical advances aside, legislation still hampered the use of steam tramway locomotives. Unaffected by the legislation was any proposed tramway that ran alongside a road. The first such line to be authorised in this country was the Wantage Tramway that connected the GWR's station of that name with the town it purported to serve, some 2½ miles distant. The line opened with horse traction on 11 October 1875, but on 1 August 1876 steam traction was introduced, using a rebuilt version of the self-contained car first tried on the London Tramways Co's line in November 1873. Four more lines opened or adopted the use of steam traction before 1880, all of which were either roadside or rural ones:

- 1877 Swansea & Mumbles Railway
- 1877 Vale of Clyde Tramways Co
- 1877 Wharncliffe National Rifle Association (Wimbledon Common)
- 1879 Guernsey Steam Tramway Co Ltd

Few towns or cities adopted steam trams before 1880 as their regular use was prevented by the laws referred to above. This was in part overturned by new legislation passed under the title of the Use of Mechanical Power on Tramways Act on 11 August 1879, which permitted steam or other mechanical trams to operate provided that:

- their engines were governed to prevent them exceeding 10mph;
- all working parts above 4in from the rails were concealed from view;
- the engine operated without blast or exhaust noises;
- the machinery was practically silent;
- no visible smoke or steam was emitted.

This new legislation effected the design of the steam tram locomotive. A typical example was 11-12ft long, around 6ft wide, depending upon the track gauge, and just over 9ft high — its total weight would be 8-9 tons. Two cylinders drove the four coupled wheels, having a wheelbase of 4ft 6in. There was a small footplate platform and a set of driving controls at each end, although the locomotives were designed to be driven with their fireboxes leading. The locomotive was completely encased in a cab, access to which was via a door at the front (firebox) end. This casing extended to within four inches of the road, thereby obscuring the wheels, motion and valve gear. Around 90gal of water was carried in a tank under the footplate, and on the roof was a condenser apparatus, consisting of four layers

of 1in diameter interconnected tubes through which the exhaust steam was admitted from the cylinders; condensed water being returned to the water tank.

Self-contained steam trams did not prove popular and it was the steam tram locomotive hauling a trailer car that became the norm in the UK, partly because it could be coupled to existing horse-drawn rolling stock. Early and experimental steam tram services almost certainly used horse trams, and the increased, and for tramway purposes 'limitless', power offered by steam tram locomotives meant that they could haul much larger trams than even teams of horses. As a result, steam tramway operators soon adopted a practice of providing increased capacity on a service by coupling two or more trams together behind a single locomotive, thereby forming small trains. The Board of Trade disapproved of this, and so to provide the same seating capacity in a single unit, larger 'trailer cars' were developed.

The first of these was introduced on 26 June 1883 for the opening of the South Staffordshire & Birmingham District Steam Tramway Co's line between Handsworth and Darlaston. Around 30ft long, these double-deck trailers

Right:
Birmingham's other steam tram operator was the Birmingham Central Tramways Co Ltd (BCT). It was the successor to a company established in 1881 that had begun to work steam trams in December 1884. The tram shown was photographed c1886 on the line to Sparkbrook, opened in May 1885. Locomotive No 57 was built by Beyer, Peacock in 1886 and trailer car No 41 was one of a batch supplied by the Falcon Engine & Car Co in December 1884. Like the Birmingham & Aston Co, the BCT used route letters, the large 'S' on the locomotive indicating the Sparkbrook route. Birmingham's last steam tram ran on 31 December 1906. *IAL*

Right:
Unlike other local authorities, Huddersfield Corporation saw the advantages of tramway operation and opted both to build and operate the tramways in their area, being the first municipality to do so. Steam trams first ran on 11 January 1883 with the opening of a service between Lockwood and Fartown. Kitson-built engine No 14 of 1888, and a trailer built by G. F. Milnes & Co in 1887, are seen in Lockwood Road. The conductor is holding a Kaye's Patent Fare Collecting Box, a device designed to foil staff from embezzling fare money. Huddersfield's last steam tram ran on 13 July 1902. *IAL*

seated around 60 and were of steel construction, having their bogies at the extreme ends for increased stability. Platforms and the lower saloon floor were on one level and the seating was longitudinal, as it was on the top deck, where the knifeboard type was used. The lower saloon was glazed and enclosed whilst the upper one had glazed end screens and an overall roof, the sides being open. As with horse trams, trailer cars were also produced with 'garden seat' type upper-deck seating from 1886 onwards, and later versions had more enclosed top decks. The largest trailer cars were produced for the Wolverton & Stony Stratford Tramway in 1888. They were 44ft long and seated 100.

The 1880s was the decade of the steam tram. Of the 50 steam tramways ever to operate in the British Isles, 45 were opened in this decade; none being opened in the 1890s. The number of steam tramways opening in each year of the 1880s was:

1880	4	1885	5
1881	6	1886	2
1882	6	1887	2
1883	7	1888	1
1884	9	1889	3

Regionally, the number of steam tramways opened during the 1880s were:

Scotland	2
North East	6
North West & Lancashire	9
Yorkshire	7
Ireland	7
Midlands	10
East & East Anglia	2
West	2
London & the South	2

showing that their greatest uptake was in the industrial centres of the Midlands, the northwest, Yorkshire and the northeast.

Most urban steam tramways operated for upwards of 20 years or more, but some were shorter-lived. The Bristol Tramways Co Ltd's steam tramway ran from the city to Horfield for just one year, from 1880 to 1881, and the Sunderland Tramways Co Ltd experimented with steam traction for some time during 1880-82. The longest continuously operating urban steam tramways were those run by the Manchester, Bury, Rochdale & Oldham Steam Tramways Co (1883-1905) and the Birmingham Central Tramways Co Ltd (1884-1906), both of which worked for 22 years. Rural lines fared even better, five lines operating with steam traction for over 40 years:

■ 43 years — Portstewart Tramway Co (1882-1925)
■ 44 years — Wisbeach & Upwell Tramway (1883-1927)
■ 49 years — Wantage Tramway Co Ltd (1876-1925)
■ 49 years — Castlederg & Victoria Bridge Tramway Co (1884-1933)
■ 52 years — Swansea & Mumbles Railway (1877-1929)

The advances in tramway technology and operating efficiency that steam haulage represented were far outweighed by the benefits of electric traction, which replaced steam trams at an increasing pace from the late 1890s. By 1900, of the 50 systems opened since 1876, 23 remained in use, but by 1905 this number had reduced to just 13, eight of which were rural lines. The UK's last urban steam tramway was the six-mile 4ft gauge Rossendale Valley Tramway, whose last car ran on 22 July 1909.

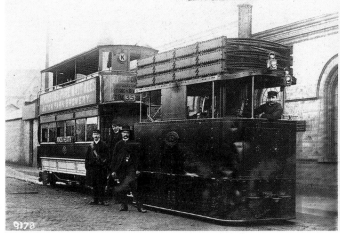

Above:
Another BCT car pictured this time inside King's Heath depot. Locomotive No 60 and trailer car No 35 are from the same manufacturers as the tram shown in the previous photograph, and the tram shows route 'K' for King's Heath. This shot affords a good view of the condenser apparatus on the roof of No 60. Typically each condenser carried about 250 thin one-inch diameter copper tubes giving collectively, a condensing surface area of around 400sq ft. *IAL*

Left:
A stunning view of Old Square, Birmingham with left, CBT locomotive No 11 *en route* to Saltley and right, Birmingham & Aston Tramways locomotive No 1 *en route* to Aston, hauling their respective trailers. Such has been the way in which Birmingham has developed during the 20th century, that all of the elegant buildings in this view have been demolished. *National Tramway Museum Collection*

CABLE TRAMS

Steam was also the power behind the other main method employed to mechanically haul tramcars — cables. Using ropes, either of hemp or wire, to haul wagons at mines or brickworks was an established technology in the 19th century. Unfortunately, the wagons or tubs pulled along by this means were attached to their ropes and either all moved or all stopped together — a system that would prove impractical if used to power street tramways. If tramcars were to use such a means of propulsion then the trams would have to be capable of being started and stopped at will, and the cable itself would have to be out of the way of other traffic.

In 1838 William J. Curtis patented a cable gripper apparatus for use on cable railways, but his ideas were not applied to tramways. Reputedly, one winter's night in 1869, Andrew Hallidie, an English-born inventor and manufacturer of wire ropes and cable-hauled mining tramways, was trudging his way up one of San Francisco's notorious hills when he came upon the driver of a heavily loaded horse tram flogging his animals to make them climb. One horse collapsed and as the driver failed to apply the car's brake, the tram rolled back to the foot of the hill, dragging its horses with it. So incensed was Hallidie that he set about devising a mechanical method of hauling trams, and what would he turn to but the technology that he knew best — cable haulage.

Hallidie's main contributions to cable tram technology were the invention of a cast-iron yoke, to provide a space beneath the street surface for the cable and the various pulleys and wheels needed to guide it, and the invention of his own grip mechanism to enable the tram to engage with or disengage from the ever-moving cable.

Andrew Hallidie first applied his inventions on the Clay Street Hill line in San Francisco, which opened on 1 August 1873. The 3ft 6in gauge line was 5,197ft long and rose 307ft in that distance. A double track was laid, the trams being former horse cars hauled by a separate gripper or 'dummy' unit. An 11,000ft steel wire rope was carried in an iron tube and supported by pulley wheels placed at 39ft intervals. The cable was wound on a drum that was turned by a steam engine at a constant speed of 6mph. From the dummy car the grip mechanism protruded down through a slot in between the running rails into a second slot in the top of the tube carrying the cable. The grip was controlled by turning a hand-wheel that had the effect of opening or closing the jaws that actually gripped on to the cable. Fourteen passengers could be seated in the trams and 16 on the dummy car, but, like steam trams, cable cars had power in abundance and loading of 70 passengers — 44 in the tram and 26 on the dummy — was not uncommon.

San Francisco's hills were suited to the use of cable trams and six more lines were opened. In the UK the cable tram was not used extensively. Only six lines were built, plus one entire system. The first cable line, indeed the first in Europe, was built in London. It was essentially a demonstration line for the Hallidie system and ran for three-quarters of a mile up Highgate Hill, where the maximum gradient was 1 in 11. The track was again 3ft 6in gauge and the line opened on 29 May 1884. Something of a novelty, this soon wore off and the line was not well used. A new company was formed to operate it, but following a serious accident in December 1892 the cars ceased to run. Passing into the hands of a third operating company, the Highgate Hill line was re-equipped and opened again in 1897, working until August 1909.

The UK's other cable tram lines were in:

- Birmingham — from the city to Hockley — opened 24 March 1888, closed 30 June 1911;
- London — from Kennington to Streatham — opened 19 December 1892, closed 4 April 1904;
- Matlock — opened 28 March 1893, closed 30 September 1927;
- Douglas, Isle of Man, the 3ft gauge Upper Douglas Cable Tramway — opened 15 August 1896, closed 19 August 1929;
- Llandudno — up the Great Orme — opened 31 July 1902, still running. The tramway has a 600ft climb in about 1 mile, maximum gradient 1 in 3.6.

Edinburgh was the only city to have a full cable tram system. The first two lines were built by the Edinburgh Northern Tramways Co and both were worked by the same winding engine. A line between Hanover Street and Goldenacre opened on 28 January 1888 and this was followed by one between Frederick Street and Comely Bank, which opened on 17 February 1890. These proved very reliable and inexpensive to operate, and when Edinburgh Corporation was looking to convert its horse tramway in the late 1890s it opted for cable rather than electric traction. The city's cable tramway system eventually covered just under 26 miles. Maintenance difficulties during World War 1 took their toll and it was decided to convert the system to electric traction. This conversion began early in 1922, the first electrified route opening on 20 June 1922 and the last cable car running on 23 June 1923.

Edinburgh's cable trams represented the only British experience of operating a cable tramway system, particularly where lines and routes had to cross each other and the cars had to negotiate curves. These inconsequential matters for horse or steam trams presented difficulties to those who engineered and drove cable trams. Common problems with cable trams were:

- breakdowns through failure of the cable, pulleys or winding engine;
- objects becoming jammed in the centre slot;
- trams stalling on curves and junctions (the cables did not run around curves and junctions, and the drivers had to release one cable, coast round, and pick up another cable);
- jammed grippers;
- frayed cables becoming caught in grippers and cars being unable to stop.

OTHER MECHANICAL TRAMS

In addition to steam and cable haulage, attempts were also made to haul or propel trams using the power of clockwork, compressed air, oil gas, coal gas and internal combustion engines. Some of these methods proved successful, and trams worked by them operated for a number of years. Other methods were just short-lived experiments, sometimes only lasting a day or so, which, none the less, have persisted into tramway folklore and gained a prominence beyond that they probably deserved.

A clockwork powered tram was built by Thomas Middleton & Co of Southwark, to designs of a Belgian,

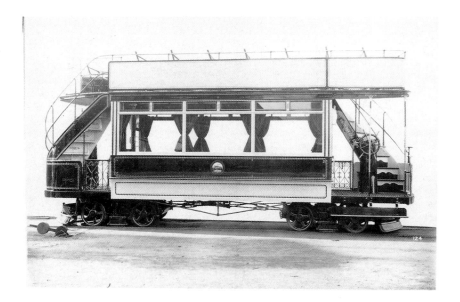

Left:
An Edinburgh & District Tramways Co cable car. Operation of the Corporation's cable tramway system was leased to this company on 9 December 1893. The company was owned by Dick, Kerr & Co of Preston, the tramcar builders. This is a makers' shot of a cable car built for the Edinburgh system. Going by the negative number, it is probably No 209 of 1903. *National Tramway Museum Collection*

Below left:
To augment their fleet of 12 double-deck cable cars the City of Birmingham Tramways purchased 10 single-deck examples, numbered 141-150. They were of an unusual crossbench, toast-rack design, ill-suited to the route or service they were operated on. Partly for this reason they saw little use and No 149 is seen in Hockley depot yard. In 1904 six of the cars were converted to electric traction, although their basic bodywork was left largely unmodified. Within three years all six cars were to be found in use on the Kinver Light Railway. *Author's Collection*

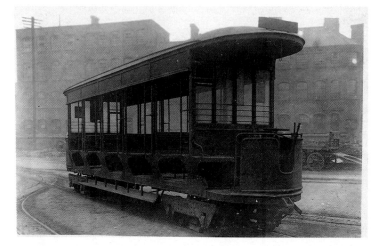

Right:
Edinburgh Corporation acquired and sold the Edinburgh Northern Tramways Co (ENT) on the same day — 1 July 1897 — the purchasers being the Edinburgh & District Tramways Co. Exactly 22 years later the latter's lease ran out and the Corporation took over the running of the cable tramways. Already committed to a programme of electrification, some of the older cable cars, notably former ENT cars Nos 121-136, were scrapped. Above, ex-ENT car No 130 is seen outside Shrubhill depot, shorn of its advertisements and awaiting its fate. *IAL*

Below right:
'The Connelly Motor' was an internal combustion engine tram built by Weymann of Guildford. It had a two-cylinder engine that ran on naphtha. Just 11ft long, the unit developed 12-13hp and was used to pull a horse tramcar. It was tried experimentally for six months spanning 1892/93 on a service run by the London, Deptford & Greenwich Tramways along Rotherhithe New Road, where it is shown in the above view. Following this trial the unit was further evaluated on services in Croydon during 1893. *National Tramway Museum Collection*

Below:
In some places, cable tramways found their niche. Lines worked with great success in Matlock, Derbyshire, and Douglas, Isle of Man, but the UK's most enduring cable tramway is the 3ft 6in gauge line running up the Great Orme in Llandudno. Built and operated by the Great Orme Tramways Co, the line rises to a height of 679ft and opened on 31 July 1902. It is operated in two sections, divided by the winding engine house at Black Gate, requiring passengers to change cars. The lower section rises 390ft, with a maximum gradient of 1:3.6, the cable being carried in a conduit slot; on the upper section the cable is exposed and runs on pulleys between the rails. In 1948 Llandudno Corporation took over the running of the tramway. Seen on 26 July 1957, cars Nos 7 and 6 pass on the upper section, with Black Gate station and engine house in the distance. The overhead wire was for signalling purposes and has been superseded by the use of radios. *Modern Transport/IAL*

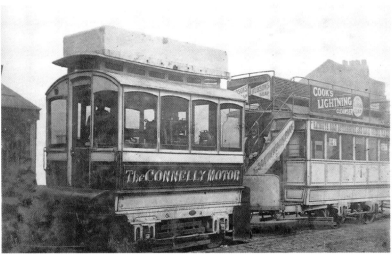

E. H. Leveaux. It hauled a horse tramcar at the Lillie Bridge depot of the Metropolitan District Railway in May 1875, attaining 7mph on a half-mile run, all on one winding. Although further experiments followed into 1876, the idea was not pursued.

Motors driven by compressed air were used to power trams running on three tramways in the 1880s:

- Wantage Tramway — from August to November 1880;
- London — King's Cross to Holloway Road — from 28 February to 16 June 1888;
- Chester — from 1886 to c1890.

The Chester experiments were by far the most extensive. They involved a self-contained double-decked tram made by the local engineering firm of Hughes & Lancaster. The four-cylinder engine used compressed air much as steam engines used steam. It was carried on board in a reservoir that could be topped up at various points from a main laid in for the purpose. When fully charged the reservoir pressure was 165lb/sq in. Unfortunately, whilst the method worked, the technology was not up to it and more air leaked out of the engine than went into powering it.

Various kinds of internal combustion engines were experimented with to power tramways, using coal gas, oil gas and petrol as their fuel. A gas-engined tram was tested in the Thornton Heath area of Croydon around October 1893, but this technology was given a fuller test in three places:

- Lytham St Annes — where a fleet of gas trams operated from 11 July 1896 to 27 February 1903;
- the Trafford Park Estate in Manchester — where gas trams were tried from 23 July 1897 and worked more or less continuously from 8 April 1898 until 1 May 1908;
- Neath, where the ex-Lytham St Annes trams worked from 1903 until 30 July 1920.

Croydon was quite a test bed for experimental means of tramway propulsion and in the six months that spanned 1892/93 'The Connelly Motor', an internal-combustion engined tram that ran on naphtha (built by Weymanns of Guildford), was tried there, but the engine ran erratically and proved unreliable. A more successful use of internal combustion engines on a tramway were the four single-deck cars operated in Heysham by the Morecambe Tramways Co. These had Leyland petrol engines and entered service in 1909, running until 24 October 1924. During World War 1 the trams were converted to run on coal gas, carried in huge balloon tanks on their roofs.

Top right:
Not one but two gas trams can be seen in front of the Trafford Park Estates Co's shed at Barton. Trafford Park's owners, impressed by the Lytham gas trams, invited their operators, the British Gas Traction Co Ltd, to provide a tramway service on a three-mile line running through the estate. After many delays a limited service began on 23 July 1897, using one car, but ceased soon afterwards. It resumed on 8 April 1898 and lasted, more or less continuously, until 1 May 1908.
National Tramway Museum Collection

Right:
Homeless after their depot blew down, the Lytham St Annes gas trams were bought for use in Neath, where they entered service later in 1903 working a four-mile former horse tram route between Briton Ferry and Skewen via Neath. Here they proved very successful and operated continuously until 20 July 1920. Car No 19 is seen at Skewen.
National Tramway Museum Collection

Bottom right:
From 11 July 1896 the Blackpool, St Annes & Lytham Tramway Co operated a fleet of gas trams between the junction of Station Road and Lytham Road, close to Blackpool South station, to Lytham. Each car seated 40 — 16 inside and 24 outside — and weighed eight tons. The engine delivered 15hp and was powered by gas pumped into on-board reservoirs at Squires Gate and Cambridge Road, Ansdell. Momentum was maintained by a large flywheel, the casing of which can be seen in between the wheels of car No 18. The service came to an abrupt halt on 27 February 1903 when the cars' wooden depot was blown down in a gale; the trams going on to work in Neath. *Author's Collection*

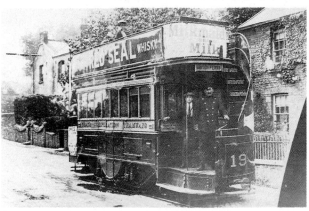

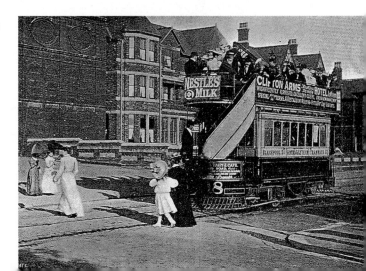

EARLY ELECTRIC TRAMS & TRAMWAY CONSTRUCTION

Whilst the notion of the electric tramway existed when tramways were first introduced in the UK, the technology to bring this about did not. The development of electric traction for tramways took place very rapidly, within the last quarter of the 19th century. When the Tramways Act of 1870 was passed no need was seen to refer to or make any provision for the electric propulsion of trams, yet by the turn of the 20th century electric trams were becoming an increasingly common sight in British streets.

THE ADVANTAGES OF ELECTRIC TRACTION

Electric traction offered a number of advantages for tramways. Horses and horse trams, for example:

- needed food and rest 24hr a day;
- had four out of five horses in the stables at any one time;
- could only work for a few years;
- could only exert a limited pull;
- had to give an excessive pull on starting-off;
- cost the same to run irrespective of the number of passengers they carried,

none of which applied to electric trams. On their own merits too, electric trams:

- were economical in the power they used, which was proportional to the work done;
- maintained higher speeds than horse or steam trams;
- used larger trams than horse trams;
- had no limit to the routes that they could work.

Many of these advantages derived from electric motors, which:

- can be overloaded to produce more than their stated output, often for long periods;
- give their maximum torque or pull on starting — the precise moment it is required;
- accelerate to a given speed quickly — vital when trams are stopping frequently.

Right:
Magnus Volk opened a quarter-mile 2ft-gauge electric railway along the seafront at Brighton on 3 August 1883, using a low, 50V current, fed through one of the running rails. This engraving, produced to publicise the line, is thought to exaggerate the luxury of the station facilities somewhat, but none the less captures the look of the line in its early, pre-third-rail days. *IAL*

Right below:
A demonstration of battery electric traction was given on 10 March 1883 when a tram designed by an Austrian, Anthony Reckenzaun, was tried on the West Metropolitan Tramways, north of Kew Bridge. Fifty accumulators, delivering a total of 107V, drove a dynamo converted to run as a motor and propelled a former horse tram along at speeds of up to 6mph. Unfortunately, later in the day a mechanical failure brought the trials to an end. The engraving above shows: (1) a general view of the tram; (2) the interior of the lower saloon, showing how the accumulators were stored under the seats; and (3) the driving controls. *National Tramway Museum Collection*

ELECTRIC MOTORS AND DYNAMOS

Electrical and magnetic phenomena were observed by peoples from ancient times, with fantastic and magical properties being ascribed to natural substances such as amber and loadstones. Wonderment at these phenomena gave way to study of them towards the end of the 16th century. Queen Elizabeth's physician, William Gilbert, embarked upon his study of magnetism in 1581, laying down its principles in his treatise *De Magnete* in 1600. What is now called 'static' electricity was the prime fascination for 17th century scientists, with no lesser luminaries than Robert Boyle, Otto von Guericke and Isaac Newton each speculating upon the nature of electrical attraction and repulsion. By the 18th century, electric current had taken over as the main subject of interest, with its principles being established through sometimes curious combinations of great minds and bizarre objects: Benjamin Franklin using kites and lightning; Aloysius Galvani prodding dissected frogs' legs with knives.

Galvani believed that electricity came from the animal tissue, but this view was challenged by Alessandro Volta, who proved that it came from a combination of certain metals and solutions, inventing the Voltaic pile — the first electric battery — in the process. Experimenting with a Voltaic pile in 1819, Hans Christian Oersted noticed that strong currents deflected a compass needle, illustrating the link between magnetism and electricity for the first time. This link was proven irrefutably by the work of Andre Ampère who, in turn, inspired Michael Faraday to repeat some of his experiments. In doing so in 1831/32, Faraday made the fundamental discovery that magnetism and electricity were different aspects of the same phenomenon and that each could be used to produce the other. The movement of a magnet within a coil of wire produced a momentary electric current, and from this discovery it was a small step to design and produce a machine that yielded an electric current in response to the application of mechanical (hand) power.

Missing from these early experiments was a ready means of demonstrating the effects of any electric current produced — the electric bell, buzzer and light bulb, so beloved of school science lessons, had still to be developed. A device that produced motion, something that everyone could see and marvel at, would be the thing, and thus it was that the electric motor came into being. Contemporary with Faraday's experiments, in the United States, Joseph Henry built a 'motor' in 1831 that rocked from side to side when a current was applied, and in Germany, Jacobi designed a motor that produced rotary motion in 1834.

There was much experimentation and refinement of the electric motor in the 1830s and 1840s, and during this period a number of people discovered that electric motors and dynamos are essentially the same machine: putting electric current into a motor produces motion and mechanical power; putting mechanical power into a motor produces electric current. Despite this, the electric motor and the dynamo were developed more or less as separate devices.

The earliest dynamos used permanent magnets and produced momentary currents that repeatedly changed direction — alternating currents (ac). In Paris on 22 September 1832, Pixii demonstrated a machine that produced a continuous or direct current (dc) through the use of a commutator. Notable work in the refinement of the dynamo was undertaken by Werner von Siemens in

Left:
Volk's Railway proved such a success that it was closed at the end of 1883 so that it could be extended and relaid to a new gauge of 2ft 9in, this being to allow for the installation of a third rail (seen to advantage in this illustration) as the means of current collection. In the 20th century Volk's Railway was extended again, to a total length of one and a quarter miles, regauged to 2ft 8½in, and modified to work at 125V. The line still runs, and is seen above in its Centenary Year, 1983, with car No 5 leaving the Easterly loop, heading towards Marine station. *Peter Groom*

Below:
The Giant's Causeway, Portrush & Bush Valley Tramway & Railway Co was an eight-mile 3ft-gauge line that used Siemens equipment and a side rail contact. Electric services began on 18 September 1883, followed by a full public service on 6 November. Use of an overhead wire method of current collection was adopted in 1899, and the line operated with few problems until it closed on 30 September 1949. In this view, taken in 1933, motor car No 9 is seen with trailers Nos 11 & 5. The notice on the car window boasts a 'HALF HOUR SERVICE EACH WAY'. Assets of the tramway were auctioned off in 25 lots on 15 March 1951, raising £11,600. *IAL*

Above:
The UK's first street running electric tramway was at Blackpool. Above, two of that town's fleet of 10 conduit trams ply their way along the seafront in the days when the buildings on the Golden Mile were still mostly houses and all still had front gardens. Blackpool's conduit tramway was officially inaugurated on 29 September 1885. The 220V current fed conductors mounted in a conduit between the running rails. Each tram carried a plough that rode in the conduit, making contact with the conductors and drawing the power off. Problems were encountered with sand and water getting into the conduit, and so it was decided to convert the tramway to an overhead wire system with effect from 13 June 1899. *W. Mate & Sons/Author's Collection*

Right:
The Bessbrook depot of the Bessbrook & Newry Tramway, a three-mile line that linked the railway station at Newry with a mill at Bessbrook. The line opened on 10 September 1885 and worked, with few problems, until 10 January 1948. An unusual feature was at Millvale, where the tramway crossed a public road. Here it used a short section of overhead wire to transmit the current, requiring the cars to carry bow collectors that were kept permanently up. *IAL*

Below:
If this illustration of the Bentley-Knight electric tramway in East Cleveland had a racehorse's pedigree, it would be called 'by artistic licence out of wishful thinking'. Services along a mile of former horse tram line converted to use Bentley & Knight's own design of conduit system, began in August 1884. Their single tramcar worked well at first, but as the rain and snow of the 1884/85 winter came along, many problems were encountered with the conduit plough and electrical shorting, which makes the impressive bow-wave shown above all the more fanciful. The Bentley-Knight East Cleveland line was abandoned after a year of intermittent operation.
University of Auburn Library, Alabama/Author's Collection

Germany, who, in 1856, devised an armature that kept its rotating coils of wire closer to the magnets in which it rotated, and Antonio Pacinotti in Italy in 1860, who made an armature that produced dc. Greatest strides were made when it was realised that the power generated was limited by the strength of the permanent magnets used, and that greater power could only be produced through the use of electro-magnets. This work was progressed through the efforts of Siemens and the British experimenters S. Alfred Varley and Sir Charles Wheatstone, each of whom unveiled dc dynamos of their own design during the latter part of 1866 and early 1867. These principles were embodied into a reliable device through the work of Zénobe T. Gramme in Belgium, who produced the first commercial dynamos in the early 1870s.

From this point larger and larger dynamos were produced, requiring the development of a means of driving them at ever higher speed. Steam engines generally produced a slow-speed rotation that could be only be used to produce higher-speed rotations through gearing or belts and pulleys. This demand produced a need for high-speed steam engines first met by the designs of Peter Willans in 1884/85 and later by the steam turbine and double-acting steam engines of the kind manufactured by Bellis & Morcom in Birmingham.

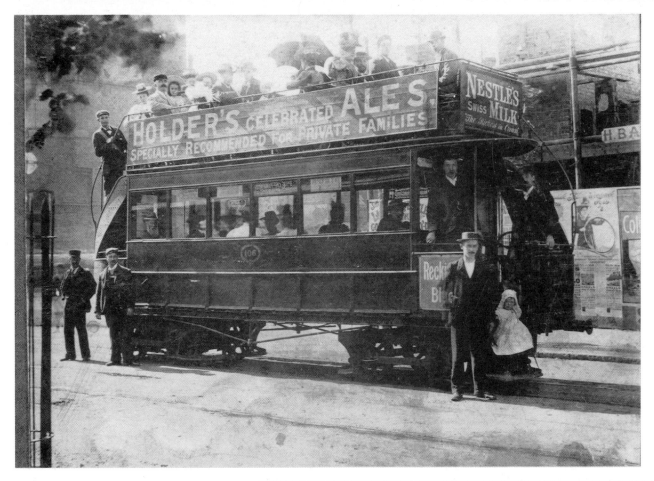

Above:
Electric accumulator trams began operation along the Bristol Road in Birmingham on 24 July 1890. A fleet of 12 cars, numbered 101-112, was used. The technology was unreliable: the batteries were heavy and often ran flat; passengers complained about choking acid fumes and 'spillages' that burned their clothing. Despite these drawbacks the trams remained in service until 13 May 1901, when they were replaced by more conventional electric trams — the longest continuous use of accumulator trams in the UK.
National Tramway Museum Collection

Right:
The Gravesend & Northfleet Tramways was effectively a 1,000yd extension to an existing horse tramway. Both types of car are seen in this engraving. It worked on an unusual 'series traction' principle in which the car, rather than completing an electric circuit, broke one. Opened for public service on 29 April 1889, the 3ft 6in gauge line presented problems with its conduit. The collector, termed the 'arrow' and seen below the driver, was an India rubber and brass composite. This repeatedly knocked down the 'spring jacks' that maintained the circuit in the conduit slot, and, combined with less than spectacular patronage, forced the line's closure in mid-November 1890.
Modern Tramway/IAL

Right:
A pair of advertisements for the Thomson-Houston Electric Co, of Boston, Chicago and Atlanta in the USA. These can speak for themselves, and clearly impressed Leeds Corporation which, with a little persuasion from one William Graff-Baker, used Thomson-Houston equipment on the electrification of the Roundhay tram route in 1891.
Author's Collection

Eckington & Soldiers' Home Railway, Washington, D.C.

The THOMSON-HOUSTON Electric Railway System in economy of operation and reliability of apparatus, possesses unquestionable features of superiority.

Out of a total of 1779 trips made during the **First** twelve days operation of the Cambridge Division of the West End Street Railway, but **Nine** trips were lost. This loss occurred on the **First** day, and was simply due to the **Inexperience of Drivers**, and in no way due to any fault of the electrical appliances.

Facts such as these prove conclusively the excellence of the apparatus.

THE THOMSON-HOUSTON ELECTRIC CO.
620 Atlantic Avenue, Boston, Mass.
148 Michigan Avenue,   Wall and Loyd Sts.,
CHICAGO, ILL.   ATLANTA, G

The Thomson-Houston Electric
RAILWAY SYSTEM.

COMPLETE, RELIABLE. ECONOMICAL.

41 Roads in Operation,
and in Process of Construction,
May 1st, 1889.

The Thomson-Houston Motors excel in qualities of Duration, Efficiency, Compactness, Easy Working, Noiselessness, and Simplicity of Construction.

The new Carbon Brushes used on the Thomson-Houston Motors cause but little wear on the Commutator, and entirely obviate any tendency to sparking.

Covered by Letters Patent and in use only on Thomson-Houston apparatus.

THE THOMSON-HOUSTON ELECTRIC CO.

EARLY EXPERIMENTS IN ELECTRIC TRACTION

Experiments with electric traction had begun in the 1830s. In 1834 Thomas Davenport, a blacksmith from Brandon, Vermont, built an electric motor that propelled itself around a 2½ft diameter circle of track, and in 1842 Robert Davidson built an electric locomotive that was demonstrated on the Edinburgh & Glasgow Railway. Both Davenport's and Davidson's vehicles carried their own battery power, but in 1847 Prof Moses Farmer built an electric car capable of carrying two people that collected its power from the running rails, like a giant model railway. Other experiments followed, but, until the perfection of the dc generator, all had to rely upon battery power that was both heavy and easily depleted. For example, Robert Davidson's vehicle was 16ft long and weighed six tons, two tons of which was the batteries, comprising some 78 individual cells, that propelled it to a maximum speed of 4mph.

Interest in electric traction waned until the mid-1870s, but a number of papers were published putting forward various designs of electric railway and tramway. During this 'interlude' some of what became the principles of electric traction were first proposed, including the fundamental one, that the tram or train should complete an electrical circuit, and the idea that electric current could be transmitted by overhead wires, with the running rails acting as the return.

Appropriately enough it was Werner von Siemens who demonstrated the first practicable application of electricity to the mass movement of people. On 31 May 1879 a 350yd-long narrow gauge line was opened at the Berlin Industrial Exhibition. A small four-wheeled locomotive, on which the driver sat, hauled three passenger cars each capable of carrying six people. A current of 150V was delivered by a third rail and returned via the running lines. This ensemble, which resembled a ride-on miniature railway, could attain 8mph and, over the period of the exhibition, carried no fewer than 80,000 passengers. Similar lines followed at other exhibitions, but an abler demonstration of vehicles in regular service was required. The town of Lichterfelde, outside Berlin, had a military academy, called the Cadet School, which was some 1½ miles from the railway station there. Siemens constructed a tramway to link the two and this came into use on 12 May 1881. With converted horse trams that could carry 26 passengers, the line used 100V that was delivered through the running rails only, complaints having been made following the number of shocks experienced at the earlier exhibition by people touching the third rail. The line worked well, unless it rained, when lying water caused spectacular short circuits between the rails.

THE DEVELOPMENT OF ELECTRIC TRACTION IN THE UK

In the UK, the years 1883-86 were to see five very able demonstrations of the effectiveness of electric traction, each using different technology, but all having one thing in common — they were built on or near to the coast. Honour of being the first goes to Magnus Volk, who opened a ¼-mile 2ft gauge electric railway along the seafront at Brighton on 3 August 1883. This used a low 50V current, fed through one of the running rails. The line proved a great success, and was closed at the end of 1883 so that it could be extended by ⅜th of a mile and relaid to a new gauge of 2ft 9in, this being to install a third rail as the means of current collection. In the 20th century Volk's Railway was extended again, to a total length of 1¼ miles, regauged to 2ft 8½in, and modified to work at 125V, but it still runs.

Both the second and third of the UK's electric lines were in Ireland. The Giant's Causeway, Portrush & Bush Valley Tramway & Railway Co was incorporated on 29 August 1880. It planned to build a tramway from the station at Portrush to Bushmills, which would then continue as a railway on to Dervock — hence the company's title. In the event the latter section was not built and the eight-mile 3ft gauge line terminated within a mile of the famous geological feature known as the Giant's Causeway. Track construction was completed by the New Year 1883 and from 29 January a passenger service was worked by steam. Electricity was generated by waterpower,

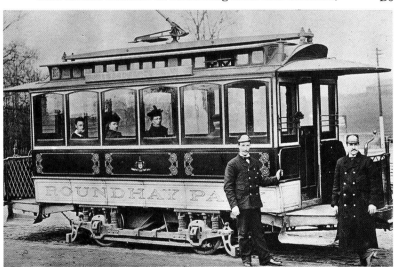

Left:
Public services on the UK's first street running overhead wire electric tramway commenced in Leeds on 11 November 1891, when a two-mile line along Roundhay Road, and a half-mile line along Harehills Road, came into use. The line was the work of an American engineer, William Graff-Baker, the vehicles being supplied by the International Thomson-Houston Co, which also supplied the overhead and generating plant. The track was owned and laid by Leeds Corporation.
Passenger Transport Journal/IAL

Left:
When it opened, on 14 July 1898, the Blackpool & Fleetwood Electric Tramroad suffered the best problem of all that the operator of a new venture of its kind could face — over patronage. There is no way that all of these people are going to fit on to one tram! The view is of Gynn station. In its first three months of operation the eight-mile tramway carried 514,000 passengers.
W. Mate & Sons/Author's Collection

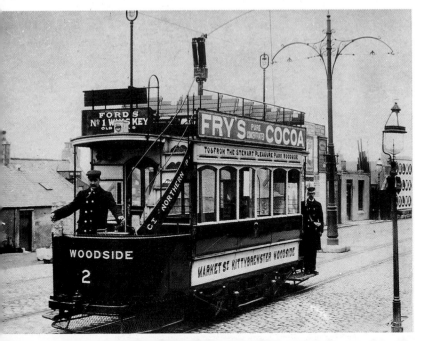

Above:

A pair of photographs illustrating some of the problems associated with electrifying an existing tramway. The scene is the Bull Ring in Sedgley, sometime during the summer of 1901. Steam trams between Dudley and Wolverhampton via Sedgley were operated by the Dudley & Wolverhampton Tramways Co Ltd, which was sold to the Wolverhampton District Electric Tramways Ltd (WDET), a subsidiary company of the British Electric Traction Co Ltd (BET), on 22 April 1899. The line was standard gauge, and later that year BET set about both electrifying it and relaying the track to the narrower, and more common Black Country gauge of 3ft 6in. The section between Dudley and Sedgley depot was completed by August 1900 and electric trams ran on this from 3 October 1900. Sedgley's Bull Ring lies north of this depot, and so a shuttle service of steam trams was maintained to Wolverhampton. The contract to relay this section was let to George Law & Co, of Kidderminster, work beginning in May 1901. Here, as a steam tram passes, Law's workers wait to erect a traction pole… *Author's Collection*

Left:

… and as soon as the tram had passed they swing the pole into place, using the BET's tower wagon No 6. Law's carts were loaded with concrete, which the workers have begun to turn over with spades in readiness for setting in the pole — much to the interest of locals. Relaying with a double line of 3ft 6in tracks followed, and the section of route from here to Sedgley depot came into use on 24 August 1901; the remainder of the route, to the Fighting Cocks in Wolverhampton, opening on 9 January 1902. *Author's Collection*

Left:

No space was wasted on Aberdeen Corporation's car No 2, seen here at Woodside terminus. The Market Street-Kittybrewster-Woodside route was the city's first electrified one and opened on 23 December 1899. This view was probably taken on a trial run made the day before the official opening ceremony. In addition to the car declaring the route information and advertisements, the box beneath the trolley pole springs bears the admonition: 'NO spitting on the car'. *Collection of the late Michael Waller/Peter Waller*

and once technical snags had been sorted out trials of the 250V electric service, which used Siemens equipment and a side-rail contact, began on 18 September 1883, followed, on 6 November, by a full public service. The line operated, with few problems, until it closed on 30 September 1949.

A similar history unfolded for the Bessbrook & Newry Tramway. Incorporated on 26 May 1884, the line linked a railway station at Newry, with a mill at Bessbrook, three miles distant. Waterpower again generated the electricity, feeding 245V from a generator at Millvale to a third rail mounted in between the running lines. The tramway opened on 10 September 1885 and worked, again with few problems, until 10 January 1948. An unusual feature of the line was a point at Millvale where it crossed a public road. Here the tramway used a short section of overhead wire to transmit the current, as the presence of a live third rail in the road was not thought safe. As a consequence of this section the Bessbrook & Newry cars carried bow collectors that were kept permanently up.

Just three weeks after the Bessbrook & Newry Tramway opened, England's second coastal electric line — the Blackpool tramway — came into use on 29 September 1885. This standard gauge conduit line ran for just under three miles, mainly along the seafront, from Cocker Street, just north of Talbot Square, to Dean Street, just north of the present South Pier. The tramway bore the stamp of a Halifax man: Michael Holroyd Smith. His first contact with Blackpool came in August 1884 when he was called in to restore a narrow gauge electric railway that had been set up in the grounds of the Winter Gardens there, which he duly did. A great proponent of electric traction, Holroyd Smith

had built his own standard gauge electric tramway at his works at Cornbrook in Manchester. On 3 October 1884 he entertained the newly-formed Blackpool Corporation Tramway Committee there. The committee was seeking the best mechanical means of propelling a new tramway destined for the town.

Impressed with what they saw, the members of the Tramway Committee, who had already visited Volk's Railway and the Giant's Causeway line, opted for Holroyd Smith's system. A new company — the Blackpool Electric Tramway Co — was formed in January 1885 and the first rail was laid on 13 March that year; the track laying being completed by the end of July 1885. Before this, on 20 July, running trials began, and the tramway was officially inaugurated on 29 September 1885. Ten trams were used. Current at 220V was fed to copper conductors mounted in a conduit beneath a slot that ran centrally in between the running rails. Each car carried a current collector or 'plough' that rode in this slot, touching the conductors and drawing off the power. The Blackpool conduit line worked well at first but problems were encountered with the conduit, especially from sand and water getting into the slot. As these problems accumulated it was decided to convert the tramway to an overhead wire system, this being effected from 13 June 1899.

Completing this quintet was the Ryde Pier Tramway, itself a pioneer of early tramway construction, which, in March 1886, began an electrified service along one of its two tracks, using a Siemens third-rail system. The second track was electrified in 1890 and the electric service ran until November 1927.

ELECTRIC TRACTION IN THE UNITED STATES

Meanwhile, in the United States, earlier pioneering efforts in electric traction finally bore fruit. In August 1884 two former patent examiners, Messrs Bentley and Knight, began operating electric tramway services along a mile of former horse tram line in East Cleveland, converted to use their own design of conduit system. At first their single tramcar worked well, but both the track and conduit were laid with wood, and as the rains and snow of the winter of 1884/85 came along many problems were encountered with the conduit plough and shorting. The Bentley-Knight line ran intermittently for a year and was then abandoned.

In the autumn of 1884 John C. Henry, an ex-telegraph operator, put his knowledge of overhead wires to good use when he opened an experimental electric tramway in Kansas. Current was distributed via a pair of overhead wires, one positive, one negative, and collected by a small pair of wheels that ran along the wires — a device known as a 'troller'. The troller was connected to Henry's 'tramcar', an old railroad wagon, by the wire that fed the current to its motor. It moved along the wires with the vehicle, but Henry had difficulty in controlling the delivery of the power to his motor and the experiment did not proceed far.

Other experiments, with electric arc lamps, led Charles van Depoele to turn his attention to street railways in 1882. Various experiments followed, including one around 1885 that involved the use of a single overhead conductor wire with a trolley wheel pressed up against and running beneath it. Despite this, van Depoele favoured the use of two wires and a troller, and in 1885 opened a very successful one-mile demonstration line in Toronto that, at its peak, carried 10,000 passengers a day. Over the next two years van Depoele opened a number of electric tramways, including ones in Montgomery, Alabama (15 April 1886), Windsor, Ontario (28 May 1886), Appleton, Wisconsin (July 1886), Port Huron, Michigan (8 October 1886), and Scranton, Pennsylvania (27 November 1886).

Another seasoned experimenter was Leo Daft, who worked for four years on various designs of electric locomotives before developing the unfortunately named 'Daft System'. This again used two overhead wires and a troller, and was employed on several lines in Connecticut cities and in New Jersey. Unfortunately, the trollers presented too many problems, not the least being that they were too free-running, failing to stop with their trams and hurtling on, snapping their umbilicals and toppling off the wires!

Left:
There was far more than just track and power equipment to install when building a tramway. A depot or series of depots was needed to house and maintain the fleet of tramcars. Some systems converted and used former horse or steam tram depots, but this too created problems. One example was on the LCC Tramways, where this temporary depot was built in Marius Road, Balham, whilst Clapham depot was rebuilt. It had four roads and was equipped with a traverser to move trams between the different roads. When Clapham depot was completed, Balham went out of use until September 1915, when it was reopened to house trailer cars. Here Class A cars Nos 22, 3, 37, and 4 protrude from beneath the depot valance, whilst horse tram No 164 has been relegated to a place outside the depot. *Author's Collection*

Left centre:
Balham depot was only intended to be temporary, but it lasted until at least the 1970s, when it was in use as a car repair garage. By contrast, the Saltaire depot of the Mid-Yorkshire Tramways Co Ltd was intended to be permanent, but lasted little more than a year! Erected in Exhibition Road, the depot had five roads and housed 10 cars. It is seen here with the main steel-frame in the course of erection. The depot opened, incomplete, on 12 July 1903, 11 days before the company's first four routes came into use. Nine months later, on 30 April 1904, the Mid-Yorkshire's assets were acquired by Bradford Corporation, which built its own depot in Saltaire, at the junction of Hirst Lane and Keighley Road, which opened in August 1904. Immediately after this the former Mid-Yorkshire Saltaire depot was demolished. *National Tramway Museum Collection*

Left below:
One of the more protracted electric tramway building schemes was that in Worcester. Known locally as the 'Electric Tramway Siege', it began shortly after the end of horse tram operation on 23 June 1903 and lasted until shortly before the commencement of electric tramway operation on 6 February 1904. So much opposition was mounted against the disruption caused by this work, that it became the subject of a highly popular series of postcards. One of these views shows an autumn 1903 photograph of track relaying over the River Severn. Former horse tram tracks can be seen to the left of the new ones. *National Tramway Museum Collection*

Although innovative and pioneering, these efforts were but a prelude to the inventive genius of Frank Sprague. A US Navy Midshipman, and a mathematical genius, Sprague was posted to Newport, Rhode Island, in 1881. There he met Prof Moses Farmer, who first drew his attention to electric transportation. In late 1882 Sprague visited London to attend the Crystal Palace Exhibition. Appalled by the fumes on the steam-hauled underground railway, he conceived the idea of the upward pressure trolley wheel. On resigning from the Navy in 1883, Sprague worked for Edison at his Menlo Park laboratories for a year before leaving to form his own firm — the Sprague Electric Railway & Motor Co — to build electric motors. Following experiments in New York, Sprague secured a contract to equip a 12-mile street railway in Richmond, Virginia, with an overhead wire system and 40 electric cars. Beset by ill health and poor contractors, especially those laying the track, Sprague opened his system on 2 February 1888 and, after initial teething troubles, it was operating well by that summer. The success of the Richmond line led Sprague to secure contracts for lines in Germany and Italy. He also went on to design electric locomotives, high-speed lifts, a multiple-unit control system for electric trains, the deadman's handle, and many other electrical devices.

LATER ELECTRIC TRAMWAY DEVELOPMENTS IN THE UK

As the 1890s approached, the UK was again the scene of great developments in electric tramways, the first of which had strong American connections. It has been noted, and is readily appreciated, that electric trams work by completing a

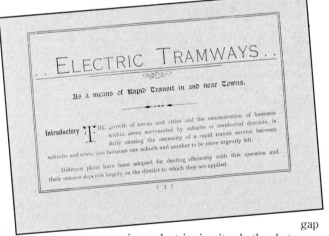

gap in an electric circuit, whether between an overhead wire and the rails, these and a third rail, or contacts in a conduit.

In theory, exceptions to this rule should not work at all, but one that did was the Gravesend & Northfleet Tramways, which used an unusual type of conduit. When no trams were operating there was a complete electrical circuit running the entire length of the line, maintained by contact plates, termed 'spring jacks', positioned every 21ft. The conduit was beneath one of the running rails, and the trams carried a plough, termed an 'arrow', made from two India rubber belts, each as long as a car. A brass strip was fastened to the outside of each belt and this acted as the electrical contact and pick-up. In operation, a wrought-iron tip on the arrow forced the spring jacks apart, breaking the electrical circuit and the Gravesend & Northfleet Tramways opened for public service on 29 April 1889. The line was 3ft 6in gauge and 1,000yd long, running along High Street Northfleet, between Station and London roads. Problems were experienced with the equipment and the conduit slot rails. These accumulated, and the line closed in mid-November 1890.

By that time a more successful demonstration of an electric tramway had also closed, but this act was predetermined. The line was built in the grounds of the International Exhibition, held at Craiglockhart in Edinburgh between 21 June and 1 November 1890. A three-quarter-mile standard gauge tramway circled the southern side of the exhibition grounds, linking stations on the Caledonian and North British railways that served the site. This tramway was unusual and important as it used an overhead wire to distribute the electric current. Two trams worked the line, each carrying a different type of trolley pole. Over the period of the exhibition, more than 15,000 people were carried on the trams.

A more permanent example of an overhead electric tramway followed a year later when the Roundhay Park Tramway opened on 29 October 1891. This line was electrified in response to an approach made to Leeds Corporation by William Graff-Baker, an American engineer and representative of the American Thomson-Houston Co. Graff-Baker offered to electrify the Roundhay tram route using an overhead wire system controlled by his company, and the city Corporation accepted. Once electrified the Roundhay line consisted of two miles of double track, running along Roundhay Road from the gates of Roundhay Park, plus half a mile of single track linking Roundhay Road with Beckett Street along Harehills Road, where a depot and generating station were built. Public services began on 11 November 1891 and used six single-decked trams supplied by the American Thomson-Houston Co.

At this point it is useful to examine how an electric

Below:
In the years immediately after opening, most electric tramways were expanded, with additional routes being constructed or original ones extended. The scene is Stafford Road, Wolverhampton in 1904, where track laying is under way on part of a new line to Bushbury. This was an extension of a line opened on 20 September 1902 to serve the Wolverhampton Wanderers ground at Molineux. Three of the system's Lorain surface contact studs can be seen in between the loop and main line placed ready for installation. The buildings to either side are part of the Great Western Railway's Stafford Road locomotive works and the notice on the railway bridge beyond is directing people to the GWR's station at Dunstall Park, opened on 1 December 1896. Trams first used the Bushbury route on 13 August 1904. *Author's Collection*

tramway worked. The following description is adapted from a number of guides that were produced to train tram drivers and was intended to be read in conjunction with the diagram reproduced here:

'The trolley wheel collects current from the overhead wire along which it rolls. This current passes through insulated wires down the centre of the trolley arm to the controller. This is a series of electrical resistances. Through it current can be completely shut off from the motors or allowed to flow in varying degree as required by the tram's speed. When starting the tram, the driver moves the controller handle notch by notch, to get a uniform rise in speed until the full current is allowed to pass through the motors. In a four-wheel tram, each axle is driven by a motor, in a bogie tram, the axles of the larger wheels are each driven by a motor. Limited space requires the motor to be as small as possible, but for a small motor to give great power it must rotate quickly. Therefore, the motor drives a large toothed wheel fixed to the axle, thus making a reduction of speed between it and the wheel. The use of two motors allows refinement of the method of tramcar control. When the current is first switched on by the controller it passes through the motors in tandem or 'series', dividing the current between them. If electric motors are to give their greatest power, or torque, on starting, they need the maximum current possible. Passing the full current through each motor in this way produces the maximum starting torque without excessive current consumption. After the tram is in motion moving to the higher notches on the controller opens up two paths for the current, one to each motor, putting them in 'parallel', so that each receives the full pressure of the current. Once the current has passed through the motors it is led to the tram's wheels and it returns through the rails, which are linked by copper bonds to form a continuous conductor.'

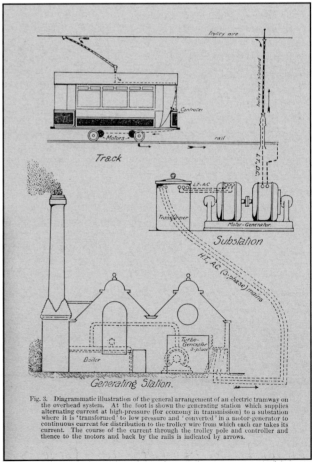

Fig. 3. Diagrammatic illustration of the general arrangement of an electric tramway on the overhead system. At the foot is shown the generating station which supplies alternating current at high-pressure (for economy in transmission) to a substation where it is 'transformed' to low pressure and 'converted' in a motor-generator to continuous current for distribution to the trolley wire from which each car takes its current. The course of the current through the trolley pole and controller and thence to the motors and back by the rails is indicated by arrows.

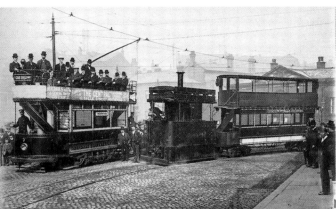

Left:
Motorman Andrew Vaughan and his conductor pose with Wolverhampton Corporation No 3 on the Bushbury route, opened on 13 August 1904. The tram had been built by the Electric Railway & Tramway Carriage Works Ltd, Preston, in May 1902 and shows the cut-out made in the bottom of the lifeguard 'feeler' beneath the main dash panel. This was to allow room for the feeler to pass over a risen contact stud should it not have retracted back to road level. *Author's Collection*

Left below:
In some places the transition from older forms of tramways to electric traction was marked with due ceremony. Here in Rochdale on 12 May 1905, the day after the last steam tram ran in service, a Bury, Rochdale & Oldham Tramway Co Ltd locomotive and trailer car were run especially from Entwhistle Road depot to be posed outside The Wellington Hotel alongside a gleaming Corporation car No 7.
National Tramway Museum Collection

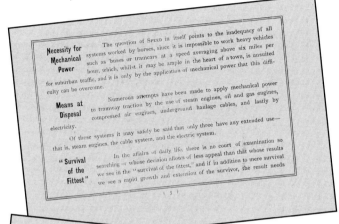

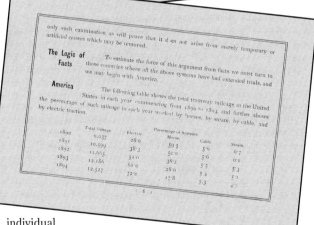

The Roundhay Park Tramway ably demonstrated the efficiency and simplicity of the overhead system. A second line using this opened on 20 February 1892, when the standard gauge Guernsey Railway, which used Siemens equipment, entered public service. Thereafter, whenever the electrification of an existing tramway was proposed or new lines promoted, the majority used the overhead system. One example was the Penarth Tramway Syndicate Ltd, which produced a detailed booklet extolling the virtues of electric tramways — reproduced throughout this chapter.

Despite the advantages of overhead wires, which included being the:

- cheapest to install;
- cheapest to maintain;
- most economical in the use of current;
- most reliable in action,

not everyone was enamoured with them. Some local authorities took great exception to overhead wires and, around the turn of the 20th century, some viable alternatives were available.

ALTERNATIVES TO OVERHEAD WIRES FOR ELECTRIC TRAMWAYS

Accumulator trams

The use of battery electric traction for tramways underwent something of a revival during the 1880s and 1890s. Developments in battery technology saw the production of storage batteries, or accumulators, that stored electrical energy in the form of chemical energy. Although individual battery cells could store and yield only a small current, connected together, lots of cells could provide sufficient power to run a traction motor. The first commercially available accumulators were produced around 1880, and it is no mere coincidence that the first accumulator-powered tram — an adapted 50-seat horse car — was put into service in Paris on 25 May 1881. That city eventually introduced accumulator trams on 19 routes, some using overhead wires whilst in the suburbs and only switching to battery power nearer to the city centre. Battery-electric traction was tried on tramways in a number of European countries during the 1880s.

In the UK, an accumulator tram was tried successfully between Stratford and Leytonstone on the North Metropolitan Tramways on 4 March 1882. Another design of accumulator car, by Anthony Reckenzaun, was tried on the West Metropolitan Tramways, north of Kew Bridge on 10 March 1883. The accumulators on this tram, as on most of the experimental battery trams, were carried under the

Above:
Passengers waiting for Chester Corporation Tramways car No 2 in Chester Street, Saltney, could amuse themselves by perusing the posters for such places as 'Laughter Land'. The date is January 1906 and this terminus by the GWR's Saltney station is typical of so many on tramway systems throughout the country at the time, when the trams had the roads to themselves. Opened on 6 April 1903, the Saltney route was one of Chester's busiest as Roodee Racecourse was situated about halfway along it. On race days trams ferried vast numbers to the races from Saltney and Chester stations. Through the bridge is the Welsh border and what was then Flintshire. *Author's Collection*

Right:
Another surface contact tramway was that run by Lincoln Corporation. This used the Griffiths-Bedell (G-B) system, and here contact studs are seen in the course of installation. The studs were extremely robust, being bedded in bitumen in a setting of solid granite. Lincoln's electric trams first ran on 23 November 1905, and the G-B worked well for 14 years. Overhead wires replaced the studs in December 1919 because, as Wolverhampton Corporation also found, the equipment was worn and the manufacturers were no longer in existence.
National Tramway Museum Collection

lower saloon seats, and were reputed to give a working period of seven hours before recharging was necessary. Other trials followed:

- February 1885 — South London Tramways, Queens Road, Battersea;
- September 1885 — Blackfriars Bridge-Clapham;
- July 1887 — Southwick-Hove;
- spring 1890 — Clapham-Tooting (six cars);
- December 1891 to January 1892 — Thornton Heath-North End, Croydon.

By far the most sustained use of accumulator trams in the UK was in Birmingham, where the Birmingham City Tramways Co introduced a service of them on a route along the Bristol Road, from the city to Bournbrook, near Selly Oak, on 24 July 1890. The cars were worked in co-operation with the Chloride Electric Syndicate Ltd, which supplied and maintained the accumulators. The cars ran for almost 11 years, giving local residents ample opportunity to experience the joys of acid fumes and spillages. The last acid-eaten Birmingham accumulator tram ran on 13 May 1901, and, apart from a few experiments at Hartlepool and in London, that was the end of accumulator trams in the UK.

Conduit systems
Mention has already been made, and the principles described, of various systems of conduit tramway. Conduit systems originated in the United States and in the 1880s, before a preferred method of current collection had emerged for tramways, they were widely used. Then they were chosen mostly for technical reasons, but after the emergence and pre-eminence of the overhead wire system, around the turn of the 20th century, conduit systems were still chosen by some local authorities and tramway operators for more æsthetic reasons, as they inherently did not require the erection of overhead wires. Notably, a number of capital cities eschewed the latter, and thus conduit tramways were to be found in both the business and administrative capitals of the USA — New York and Washington DC — as well as in Berlin, Brussels, Budapest and Paris. To that list must also be added the name of London, which had possibly the best known conduit tramway system of all.

A late-comer to the use of the conduit system, in 1900 the London County Council (LCC) was preparing to electrify its tramways. Put off the use of overhead wires, it was experimenting with a conduit system of its own devising. At that year's Tramways Exhibition, held at the Royal Agricultural Hall in London from 25 June to 4 July, the Westinghouse Co demonstrated a section of conduit track. Impressed, the LCC requested a more detailed examination of the system, which was held on 14 February 1901 on a specially constructed length of track laid in the yard of an old depot in Camberwell. Further trials followed and the LCC chose to use the system Westinghouse had demonstrated, which was in fact produced by J. G. White & Co, and already used in New York, Washington DC and Paris.

The White system used either a side or centre slot, and a 3ft 6in gauge tramway, using a combination of these slot positions, had come into use in Bournemouth on 23 July 1902. White's engineers worked with the LCC to modify their system for use in the city. A centre slot position was chosen, and various modifications were made to the cast-iron frames or 'yokes' that formed the conduit and supported the conductor or 'T' rails. The first LCC route to be electrified using this conduit system ran from the south end of Westminster Bridge to Tooting, via Kennington, Clapham and Balham. It was opened, with great ceremony, by the then Prince of Wales on 15 May 1903. On subsequent routes further modifications were made to the basic LCC conduit design. A major one involved redesigning the yokes; instead of being attached to the track by tie-bars, every alternate yoke now had long side arms that also supported the running rails.

To draw power from the conduit, tramcars were fitted with a removable collector or 'plough'. The 'T' rails were 13in below the road surface and 6in apart, and the ploughs were borne in a 'plough carrier', formed as part of a bogie casting or mounted to the underside of a tramcar, between the wheels or bogies. Although just under 2ft in length, with all the contacts and strengthening attached to them, each plough weighed around half a hundredweight. Eventually, the LCC conduit system extended to around 123 route miles. Later, less sensitive route extensions into the suburban areas were constructed using overhead wires, requiring a change from the conduit to the overhead collection systems for all trams working through. These were effected at change pits, 21 of them in all on the LCC tramways, where overhead and conduit overlapped for a short distance and the slot moved from between the rails to outside of them, either ejecting a plough or allowing the insertion of one.

Right:
Tramway points and crossings were a specialist product and the province of a small number of highly skilled manufacturers such as Hadfields Ltd of Sheffield and F. H. Lloyd & Co Ltd of Darlaston in the Black Country. This is a page from one of Lloyd's catalogues published in 1907. The photograph highlights the point of maximum wear on the crossing, where a manganese or solid cast steel insert was used to make the track harder wearing. *Author's Collection*

Below:
Laying tramway permanent way was labour-intensive, and none more so than the LCC's conduit track. In 1906 a gang of workers are laying-in (or sitting in) pointwork in York Road, Wandsworth, just south of Wandsworth Town station. The track is of what could be termed the 'Mark I' variety, that using short conduit yokes, seen clearly in the foreground. These were attached to the running lines by tie-bars, seen behind the seated worker, but were superseded by long yokes with arms cast on to support the rails. The conductor or 'T' rails ran in the centre of the space formed by the yokes. This section of track came into use on 5 August 1906. *Author's Collection*

Surface contact systems

Vying with conduit current collection as overhead-free methods were various surface contact systems. In a literal sense, any third-rail method of current collection could be classed as a form of 'surface contact' system, as that is the principle upon which it works, but with tramways the term has a more specific meaning. Essentially, all the rival systems shared a common principle — that of a series of electrified contact 'studs' located centrally in between the running rails and flush with the road surface. The underneath of each tram carried two magnets, one at each end, and a long flat electrical contact called a 'skate'. As the latter was longer than the space between the studs, in theory it was always in contact with at least one of them. In use, as a tram moved over a stud the polarity of the leading magnet raised it, causing it also to become live with current, which was picked up by the skate. As the trailing magnet, whose polarity was opposite that of the leading one, passed over the stud it returned to the level of the road surface and became electrically dead once more.

There were three leading surface contact systems used on tramways in the UK: the Lorain or Brown System, the Dolter System, and the Griffiths-Bedell System. The Lorain System was invented by William Brown in 1898 for use on underground railways in the USA. Its patent rights were taken over by the Lorain Steel Co of Pittsburgh, and thereafter the system bore their name rather than its inventor's. In the UK the Lorain system had a solitary but able demonstration in Wolverhampton, where a series of routes, opened from 26 March 1902, used it for almost 20

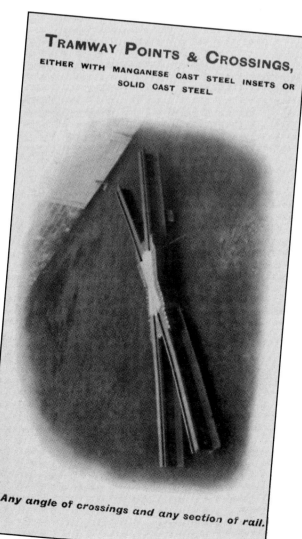

TRAMWAY POINTS & CROSSINGS, EITHER WITH MANGANESE CAST STEEL INSETS OR SOLID CAST STEEL.

Any angle of crossings and any section of rail.

years. Studs were placed at 10ft intervals and the skate beneath the cars was 14ft long. The unavailability of spare parts was among the reasons given for the conversion of the whole Wolverhampton system to overhead wires between 26 March and 15 October 1921.

The Dolter System was favoured by tramways operated by the National Electric Construction Co. Here the studs were spaced at 9ft intervals and the trams carried skates that were 12ft long. Its most successful use was on a section of the Hastings Tramways that ran along the seafront. This opened on 31 July 1905, and use of the studs was not abandoned until 1914. The least successful application of the Dolter System was on the Mexborough & Swinton Tramways, where the studs were in use only between 6 February 1907 and 30 July 1908. A combination of faulty installation, mining subsidence and methane seeping in from mine workings, ensured that whatever the date it was always 5 November when travelling on the Mexborough & Swinton Tramways. Little more success was found with the system when it was tried at Torquay. From its opening on 4 April 1907 problems were experienced with sand in the studs, and in bad weather rain and snow also wreaked their own havoc. Use of the system was abandoned in March 1911.

The Griffiths-Bedell System was invented by Benjamin Bedell, who was backed financially by William Griffiths. It was installed at Lincoln, coming into use on 23 November 1905. The studs were extremely simple, having only one moving part, and they lay flush with the road surface rather than projecting slightly above it as those of the other systems did. In Lincoln the Griffiths-Bedell System worked well and it was replaced, in December 1919, only because it was in a poor state of repair, and because the supplier had long gone out of business.

TRAMWAY CONSTRUCTION

Having opted for a system of current collection, all that a tramway operator had to do was install it. Tramway construction deserves a book in its own right, but even an outline of its stages serves to illustrate the planning, labour and expense involved before an electric tramway could be operated. Starting with an existing horse or steam tramway represented little saving in time or cost. Horse tram rails were too light for heavier electric trams, and, like steam tram lines, were also unbonded, ie not connected sufficiently well to form part of an electric circuit. In either case, existing lines would probably be too worn for reuse.

Tramway construction fell into five general stages:

1. Planning the tramway
- Choosing the system of electricity distribution — overhead wires, conduit, surface contact, etc;
- Choosing the gauge of the track — partly determined by the street width;
- Choosing the routes the tramway would run along;
- Arranging the track network to serve these routes;

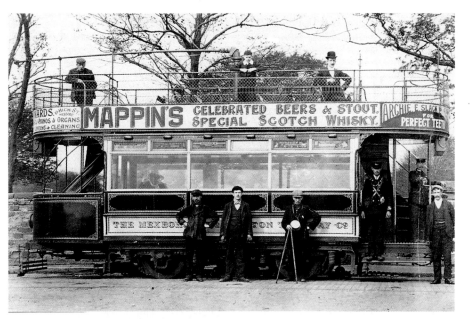

Left:
Three of the studs from the Dolter Surface Contact System used by the Mexborough & Swinton Tramways Co can be seen set in the centre of the track running in front of one of their cars. The Dolter studs gave problems from the opening of the tramway on 6 February 1907, due in part to poor installation, mining subsidence and leaks of methane from old mine workings. Journeys on the tramway were alleged to be spectacular, but not for those of a nervous disposition. Studs were also left raised and live, and the whole installation proved so problematic that it was converted to overhead wires from 30 July 1908 — after just 16 months — one of the replacement cars is shown. Trams continued to run over Mexborough & Swinton system until 10 March 1929. *IAL*

Left below:
Opposition to overhead wires from local residents forced the Torquay Tramways Co Ltd to opt for using the Dolter Surface Contact System. The track was 3ft 6in gauge and a circular route was built to Babbacombe with a branch to Torre station. Public services began on 7 April 1907, but three days earlier there was an Opening Day ceremony, with three of the fleet's 18 cars in view. The brushes beneath the lifeguard feelers are to keep the tops of the studs clear. *Author's Collection*

- Positioning the rails in streets — whether to use single or double track;
- Positioning stops & passing places along the routes;
- Siting and planning the termini;
- Siting the points & crossings in the track.

2. Constructing the permanent way
- Choosing the weight & size of rails to be used;
- Selecting a means of supporting and fixing the rails;
- Deciding how to form rail joints — with fishplates, anchors or by welding, and then doing so;
- Choosing the spacing and use of tie-bars — used to maintain the track gauge, and fitting these;
- Choosing the type of foundations and paving to use with the trackwork, and then installing them;
- Laying in the points.

3. Railbonding & welding
- Deciding whether to use the track as the return conductor — if not, making alternate arrangements for this;
- Choosing and installing the railbonds — Old style, Brooklyn, Chicago, Crown, Neptune, Columbia, Plastic, etc — to form the return circuit;
- Welding the track — choosing whether to use Falk Cast, Thermit, Electric, or Arc methods to do this — then doing so.

4. Laying in the power distribution system
- Laying in the power feeder cables;
- Laying in the return circuit;
- Positioning the section pillars to divide the power distribution system into sections — usually of half a mile.

5. Installing the overhead
- Choosing the system of overhead to use;
- Excavating the holes for the traction poles — 6ft or so deep;
- Installing the traction poles at their correct rake — they should lean back when they do not carry any load, and be pulled nearly vertical by the weight and tension of the overhead wires;
- Erecting the traction poles and their fittings;
- Erecting the trolley wire;
- Putting tension into the trolley wire;
- Installing the overhead wire fittings — line ears and frogs, etc — where the wires are suspended from and above points in the trackwork;
- Installing guard wires to prevent telephone wires and telegraph cables from falling on to the live tramway overhead.

This long and involved process meant that town and city streets were often taken up for weeks and months on end. Considerable disruption was caused to general and commercial life whilst this was happening, and this period was referred to as the 'Tramway Siege' or 'Tramway Occupation'. Traders sometimes sued tramway companies for loss of income, often prejudicing attitudes to the new tramways, which were branded a 'nuisance' or 'menace' before they had even had a chance to demonstrate their benefits. Times and people do not change, and the citizens of Manchester and Sheffield experienced these same problems, with similar reactions, in the early 1990s.

Top:
Torquay's experience with the Dolter system was little better than Mexborough & Swinton's. This 'Snowed Up' postcard view above may have been posed, but the sentiment would have struck a chord with many of the tramway's unfortunate passengers. Later in 1910, it was decided to build a line to Paignton, for which use of the overhead wire system was adopted. Conversion of the original system therefore became more or less inevitable. The conversion was completed by 6 March 1911 and the Paignton route opened four months later, on 17 July. Torquay's last tram ran on 31 January 1934. *Author's Collection*

Above:
Electric tramways took root in many different kinds of area, including the industrialised valleys of South Wales, where urban and rural landscapes nestled cheek-by-jowl. Above is the scene on the opening day of the Rhondda Tramways Co Ltd — 11 July 1908. The tramway ran between Trehafod and Partridge Road, Rhondda Fawr, and Pontygwaith in Rhondda Fach. A rather top-heavy car No 1 is being given a somewhat muted send-off by a crowd who seem more interested in the camera. *C. Batstone*

Below:
The rural aspect of the Rhondda Tramways Co Ltd's system is seen is this view of car No 13 on the Tonypandy route. Tram crew outnumber the solitary passenger two-to-one. *C. Batstone*

Above:
London's first regular electric tramcar services were provided by London United Tramways (1901) Ltd, which opened three routes — Hammersmith-Kew Bridge, Shepherds Bus-Acton and Shepherds Bus-Kew Bridge — on 4 April 1901. Seen at the company's Chiswick depot, an immaculate car No 90 was one of an initial batch of 100 Class Z trams ordered for the opening of the tramway. *London Transport*

Right:
The Rhondda Tramways prospered in the years before World War 1, and the development of the motorbus that would follow it. New routes were built: a line to Porth opened on 5 November 1908; and another from there to Maerdy in April 1912. Here, Rhondda Tramways car No 23 is seen leaving Porth Depot *en route* to Maerdy. This was a golden period for electric tramways; in a few years' time they would not have the roads all to themselves. *Michael Dunne*

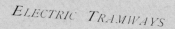

ELECTRIC TRAMWAYS

AS A MEANS OF RAPID TRANSIT IN AND NEAR TOWNS.

Entered at Stationers' Hall. Copyright the property of I. B. Atkinson Co.

Description of the System
An electric car is a car fitted with a machine called an electric motor, which, when supplied with an electric current, produces motive power to turn the wheels and so move the car. This electric current may be supplied by electric accumulators or storage batteries carried on the car, charged at intervals, and lasting till the charge is run out; but this system has not so far proved successful.

Another system is by the use of conductors or metallic strips, laid in a channel under the road, with a slot as in the cable system, through which a tongue or plough passes, which, making contact with the conductors, picks up the electric current at each point of its passage, the electric power being derived from fixed engines and dynamo electric machines in a generating station or power house. This system has the objections of the slot in the road and its considerable constructional cost. It is in successful operation in this country, and some few other places.

... united electrical system is that of supplying ... ngside of the tramway, which is

connected with the electric motor on the car by a pole or mast with a wheel or trolley on the top, running on and guiding itself along the wire all the way. This is known as the overhead or trolley system.

How this meets the case
By this means the engines developing the necessary mechanical power may be situated where most convenient, that is, where land and fuel are convenient and cheap, and where the works will occasion no nuisance. The power is transmitted by means of an electric wire, noiselessly and without even being apparent. The motor under the car is comparatively light, is unseen, is almost noiseless, and gives off no fumes or vapours. The car may be run at a slow speed in the town and faster in the suburbs, whilst the same electric current is used to heat the car in winter and to light it brilliantly after dark.

What are we waiting for?
This question may well be asked, and may be readily answered. There has been until recently a prejudice in this country against overhead wires, causing a difficulty in obtaining the consent of the road authorities to the erection of this necessary adjunct to the system.

DECORATED TRAMS –
OVERTURE AND BEGINNERS PLEASE

Freed from any obvious and distracting form of haulage, and supplied with an abundance of power, electric trams lent themselves to being decorated for special occasions. Being rail-borne they were also capable of being disguised as other things to a far greater extent than other road vehicles, where the maintenance of good visibility for the driver was far more important. Decoration took many forms, but the most striking effects could be obtained through the use of lots of electric light bulbs. Opportunities to produce decorated trams were many and varied, ranging from national celebrations of Coronations and Jubilees, VE Day etc, to purely local events such as anniversaries or charitable drives. The first occasion upon which electric trams had the opportunity to 'put on a show' was appropriately enough, at their opening ceremonies.

Above:
Just about every part of these Leyton Corporation trams that could have something either wound round it or hung from it seems to have enjoyed the privilege, as garlands, bunting, drapes, assorted vegetation and many light bulbs adorn the trams in this cavalcade. It is the Opening Ceremony for Leyton's almost nine miles of tramway, which took place on 1 December 1906. The cars are lined up in fleet order, the leading one is No 20, the next No 21, and so on. Only 15 years later the system was so run down that an agreement was struck with the LCC Tramways to operate it on the Corporation's behalf. *Author's Collection*

Left:
At the ceremonial opening of the Dundee, Broughty Ferry & District Tramways, on 27 December 1905, a patriotic theme was adopted. Three cars, in all their finery, were lined up at Milton, as shown here. Bunting was applied to the decency panels, the front car, No 3, sporting red, the second car white, and the third car blue. The weather looks wet, and the contrast between the paved surface of the tramway and the road and paths around is striking. For most of its working life the tramway had only 14 trams, the last to run did so on 15 May 1931. *The late Michael Waller/Peter Waller*

ELECTRIC TRAMS TO 1919

Despite the upheavals inherent in converting or constructing a tramway for electric traction, many local authorities and private companies did so. By 1910, there were over 300 separate tramway undertakings in the UK, 134 of which had been opened during the preceding decade:

Above:
By 1910 most towns and cities that were going to have electric tramways already had them, but not York. The city was a comparative late-comer to the advantages of electric traction and retained its horse trams until this time. Road upheavals, of a kind that were fading in most people's memories, are seen by Micklebar Gate in the city during 1909. Electric trams first ran on 20 January 1910, and York's last tram ran on 16 November 1935. *Author's Collection*

YEAR	NUMBER OF ELECTRIC TRAMWAYS OPENED
1900	10
1901	29
1902	19
1903	24
1904	22
1905	12
1906	9
1907	4
1908	3
1909	2

Above:
A number of tramway operators experimented with the type and quality of service they provided. Liverpool Corporation provided First Class trams on routes serving better-off suburbs between 1908 and 1923. For a premium fare passengers were spared having to mix with any 'working people'. The tram illustrated, London United Tramways No 175, was built as a double-decker but converted to this form in 1911. It was a Private Hire car, let out to parties wishing 'to attend the theatre or other entertainments'. Inside had pile carpet, velvet curtains and vases of flowers. Chairs were loose, and the car could seat 20, or 16 if an optional buffet, set up at one end, was chosen. No 175 was first hired for a wedding on 23 September 1911.
London Transport Executive

Right:
In a way, all of Edinburgh's trams would remain cable-hauled until 1922, even though the Corporation built a short electric traction line in 1910. This ran along Slateford Road from Ardmillan Terrace and opened on 8 June 1910. It was operated on the Corporation's behalf by the Edinburgh & District Tramways Co. The trams were converted cable cars and had their controllers at the side of each platform rather than in front. If there doesn't appear to be any overhead in the above view, taken at or near to the opening, then there probably isn't — the line was so isolated that the trams had to be hauled to and from Shrubhill depot by cable cars! *IAL*

Yet, even before this decade had ended, the rate at which new electric tramways were being built had tailed off dramatically, particularly after 1904. In the following decade new electric tramways were few and far between, with only five opening in the years 1910-13, and none thereafter. These new tramways were:

■ York Corporation Tramways — 20 January 1910
■ Llanelly & District Electric Lighting & Traction Co — 16 January 1911
■ Grimsby & Immingham Electric Railway — 15 May 1912
■ Nottinghamshire & Derbyshire Tramways Co — July 1913
■ Aberdare Corporation Tramways — 9 October 1913.

What were the reasons for this sudden decline? A number of explanations are possible, including competition from the up and coming motorbus, and the first experiments with trolleybuses, but the most compelling factors underlying this trend are financial. A form of Tramway Mania existed in the UK at the turn of the 20th century, during which electric tramways were built in places where, perhaps, they should not have been. Once built, these tramways would have been expected to:

■ pay their running costs;
■ repay the loans taken out to build them;
■ provide a dividend for their shareholders.

Sadly, some tramway operators found that forecast passenger numbers did not materialise, and the grumbles of dissatisfied shareholders and councillors gifted with hindsight began to feed back into the movement, stymieing its progress. Stuck to the routes where their tracks had been laid, at great expense, trams started to be seen as inflexible, creating a niche for a more flexible form of public transport.

Much of the development of the motorbus took place in London, where such a niche already existed, although the British Electric Traction Co (BET), the parent company for a number of provincial tramways, became interested in them too, and was involved in producing experimental designs for both bodies and chassis through a specially formed subsidiary company - the British Automobile Development Co. A 3½-ton unladen weight restriction, imposed by the Metropolitan Police, also spurred bus operators on to produce lighter designs.

Reliable lightweight motorbuses, such as the London General Omnibus Co's 'B'-type, that used standardised and interchangeable parts, had been developed by 1912, and with a seating capacity of 34 they began to be seen as viable alternatives to trams on lighter loaded journeys. When the Sheerness & District Electric Power & Traction Co's tramway service ended on 7 July 1917 — the UK's first electric tramway abandonment — its trams were replaced by motorbuses.

Opposite above:
The BET Co held extensive tramway interests in the Midlands. One of their subsidiary concerns was the Potteries Electric Traction Co Ltd, whose 32-mile network of 4ft 0in gauge lines linked the Five Towns in the Stoke-on-Trent area. Car No 95, photographed on the Stoke and Trent Vale route around 1910, was typical of the large single-decked bogie tramcars favoured by the company. Displaying the route in this position was unusual. BET had interests in few 4ft 0in gauge tramways. One such was at Barrow-in-Furness, where two Potteries cars were sold in 1915. *IAL*

Opposite below:
Wolverhampton Corporation's Lorain surface contact system was working at its peak when this view was taken of cars Nos 6, 10 and 11 in Tettenhall Road. The combination of the trees, the absence of overhead wires and of other traffic, makes for a very pleasing scene. *National Tramway Museum Collection*

Above:
Some routes serving Wolverhampton were worked by the Wolverhampton District Electric Tramways Ltd (WDET), a BET subsidiary. Car No 19 is seen at Darlaston Bull Stake terminus, around July 1914, waiting to depart for Willenhall from outside John Mason's newsagent's shop. The newspaper headlines are reporting trouble in Ireland, but other problems would soon grip the nation. Over on the left, beneath the lamps and finger-posts, are some clock faces, used to show the times of the next tram departures. The large number 6 indicates the fare stage on the tram route. Unusually for a BET subsidiary, this WDET car does not appear to be displaying the company's 'Magnet & Wheel' symbol. *Author's Collection*

The trolleybus was developed in Germany and France. Using electric traction, it ran on the road rather than in rails. Twin overhead wires were needed, one for the current supply, another for its return. Before the now familiar name was coined for these vehicles they were more descriptively termed 'Railless Traction' or 'Trackless Trolleys'. Twin schemes, in Leeds and Bradford, inaugurated the UK's first trolleybus lines on 20 June 1911, and before 1920 nine more would follow:

- Dundee — 5 September 1912
- Rotherham — 30 October 1912
- Stockport — 10 March 1913
- Keighley — 3 May 1913
- Ramsbottom — 14 August 1913
- Aberdare — 7 October 1913
- Rhondda — 22 December 1914
- Mexborough & Swinton — 31 August 1915
- Teesside — 8 November 1919

None of these trolleybus schemes replaced tram routes; they were used to augment existing services or to provide new ones.

Without World War 1, the development and wider spread use of both the motor and trolleybus would have continued to gain pace, but the hostilities put most of this on hold until the 1920s.

CAR & CANAL, KINVER.

Opposite above:
From 1 August 1908 the Mexborough & Swinton Traction Co used a conventional overhead wire system in place of the Dolter surface contact studs that had proved so problematic in operation. Car No 18 is seen in High Street, Rawmarsh, at the top of Rawmarsh Hill. A low bridge required the base of the car's trolley pole to be fitted on the side of the roof. When the last Mexborough & Swinton tram ran on 9 March 1929, the services were taken over by trolleybuses. *Author's Collection*

Opposite below:
Commercial photographs featuring trams were usually taken for use on postcards as shown here. This unusually expansive photograph dates from 1916 and comes from a catalogue produced by a road surface treatment manufacturer. The scene is Barrow-in-Furness, where the 4ft 0in gauge tramways were worked directly by the BET Co. Car No 20 of 1910, a 96-seater, and is seen on Walney Bridge approach, passing between the massive shops of the Vickers Armstrong shipyard. The route, over an opening bridge to Walney Island, opened on 8 June 1909. Barrow's tramways were taken over by the Corporation from 1 January 1920, the last tram running on 5 April 1932.
Author's Collection

Above:
Few tramways could compete with the BET-owned Kinver Light Railway (KLR) for the scenery to view on the line. The second half of the four-mile journey was entirely cross-country, as the tramway threaded its way in between and over the River Stour and Staffordshire & Worcestershire Canal. Here tram No 46, one of the original cars bought for the opening of the line, is seen passing Hyde Meadow. An eight-car depot was situated in the trees just behind the car. *Author's Collection*

Below:
Car No 48 was a sister to Nos 46 and 47, and is seen at the KLR's Kinver terminus. They were built as double-deckers but when the line was inspected by the Board of Trade on 1 April 1901 the inspector came out against the use of such cars. Stuck without any trams with which to open their new line, the KLR took the drastic step of hurriedly removing the top decks. The last of the three cars to remain in service, No 48 was fitted with a central bulkhead, around 1912, to provide smoking and no smoking accommodation. *Ron Thomas Collection*

Above:
This surprisingly modern view of Swindon Corporation tramcar No 4
approaching a terminus comes from the same catalogue mentioned
on P. 49. Here one is supposed to be admiring the 3ft 6in gauge track's
foundations. Swindon's tramway exemplifies many small systems built at
the height of the Tramway Mania: 3.7 route miles to cover three basic
routes, with a maximum fleet of 13 cars. The system opened on
22 September 1904 and closed on 11 July 1929. *Author's Collection*

A BIT ON THE SIDE – TRAMWAY ADVERTISING

Advertisements carried on tramcars were an attractive source of income for tramway operators and brought some diversity to otherwise uniform vehicles for the travelling public. For tramway enthusiasts too, the advertisements carried on trams have become a ready means of identifying where a particular photograph was taken. Indeed, one sometimes wonders if it was only Londoners who enjoyed '…and Hovis and butter for tea', and only the citizens of Sunderland who could 'Shop at Binns'.

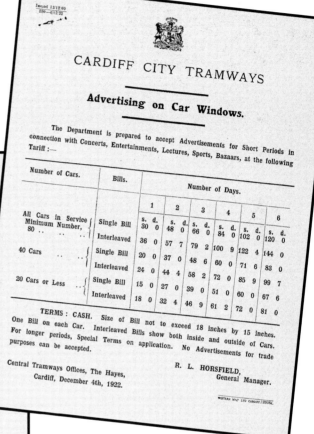

CARDIFF CITY TRAMWAYS

Advertising on Car Windows.

The Department is prepared to accept Advertisements for Short Periods in connection with Concerts, Entertainments, Lectures, Sports, Bazaars, at the following Tariff :—

Number of Cars.		Bills.	Number of Days.					
			1	2	3	4	5	6
			s. d.	s. d.	s. d.	s. d.	s. d.	s. d.
All Cars in Service Minimum Number, 80	{	Single Bill	30 0	48 0	66 0	84 0	102 0	120 0
		Interleaved	36 0	57 7	79 2	100 9	122 4	144 0
40 Cars	{	Single Bill	20 0	37 0	48 6	60 0	71 6	83 0
		Interleaved	24 0	44 4	58 2	72 0	85 9	99 7
20 Cars or Less ..	{	Single Bill	15 0	27 0	39 0	51 0	60 0	67 6
		Interleaved	18 0	32 4	46 9	61 2	72 0	81 0

TERMS : CASH. Size of Bill not to exceed 18 inches by 15 inches. One Bill on each Car. Interleaved Bills show both inside and outside of Cars. For longer periods, Special Terms on application. No Advertisements for trade purposes can be accepted.

Central Tramways Offices, The Hayes, Cardiff, December 4th, 1922.

R. L. HORSFIELD, General Manager.

A PAPER ON
RAIN=PROOF SEATS
FOR TRAMWAY CARS AND OMNIBUSES ;
ALSO ON
Outside Signal Bells
FOR THE USE OF PASSENGERS ON TRAMWAY CARS & OMNIBUSES.

CLIFTON SUSPENSION BRIDGE. FARE 1d

TRAMWAYS CENTRE

13

With incidental reference to
Supplementary and Emergency Brakes
BY
C. CHALLENGER,
Traffic Manager of the Bristol Tramways & Carriage Co., Ltd.

BRISTOL:
EDWARD EVERARD, PRINTER & PUBLISHER.
1896.

Above:
Advertisements large and small were carried on tramcars. This tariff sheet was published by Cardiff City Tramways in December 1922 and is self-explanatory. Just £6 to promote the Church Bazaar on every Cardiff tram for a week isn't bad. The General Manager went on to the same post in Leeds, where his name was perpetuated as that for a class of tramcars completed after his death in August 1931.
Andrews Collection/Glamorgan Record Office

Left:
Tramcars also featured in advertisements. This illustration has something of a cartoon feel about it: Lady on Top Deck of Tramcar: 'Excuse me Sir, have you seen Mr. Challenger's excellent paper on Rain-proof seats for Tramway Cars and Omnibuses?' Gentleman: 'No, I haven't Madam. I'm more concerned with what that fellow up there is doing with his sketch pad!'. Mr Challenger wasn't superstitious either; a full Bristol horse car No 13 models his rain-proof seats. It isn't known how successful these seats were at repelling the rain, but demand for them would soon be drastically reduced through the designs of a Mr Bellamy of Liverpool.
Andrews Collection/Glamorgan Record Office

Right:
If a tramway undertaking did not want to have the responsibility of letting advertisements on its vehicles, this work could be handled by an advertising agent who paid them a percentage of the charges levied. There were two main agencies in this market: Griffiths & Millington Ltd, and — as seen above in their own advert from 1932 — Darby's Advertising Agency Ltd. *Author's Collection*

Below:
Perhaps the number 13 was considered lucky in advertisements featuring trams; here it is again in this 1936 London Transport plea for clients to fill up the Tram Sides and Dash Boards of its tramcars. A quick tot-up with a pencil, paper and fleet list ought to show how much it cost to promote all that Hovis. *The Railway Magazine/Author's Collection*

CONTRACTORS
FOR
ADVERTISING
ON
TRAMCARS
AND
OMNIBUSES

DAA

DARBY'S
ADVERTISING AGENCY LTD

AUSTRALIA HOUSE, Strand, LONDON, W.C. 2
Telephone—Temple Bar 9087 (2 lines)   Telegrams—"Darbadvert, Estrand, London"
and at 97 SHIRLEY ROAD, CROYDON
Telephone—Addiscombe 3147 (2 lines)   Telegrams—"It, Croydon"

WE OFFER THE
HIGHEST
POSSIBLE
RENTAL
FOR ANY SYSTEM
OF
TRAMS OR BUSES.

Make your advertising EFFECTIVE

Take prominent positions

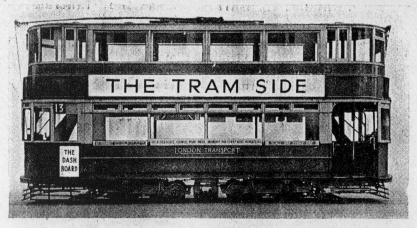

THE TRAM SIDE

LONDON TRANSPORT

THE DASH BOARD

TRAM SIDES
(SIZE 20' × 20")

5/- per week

DASH BOARDS
(SIZE 20" × 30")

1/6 per week

Enquiries to Commercial
Advertising Officer
55 Broadway, S.W.1
VICtoria 6800

LONDON TRANSPORT

ELECTRIC TRAMS TO 1929

The trends and developments in the provision of public road transport that had begun before World War 1 resumed, continued and gained pace throughout the 1920s.

There were only three tramway electrification schemes during the decade:

- Edinburgh Corporation Tramways — 20 June 1922
- Dearne & District Light Railways — 14 July 1924
- Swansea & Mumbles Railway Ltd — 2 March 1929.

In Edinburgh, electricity replaced cable haulage, and in Swansea it displaced steam; the Dearne lines being the only completely new tramway system.

Tramway patronage reached an all time high during the financial year 1927/28, when trams carried an astonishing 4,705,842,932 passengers over an equally amazing 396,554,545 miles. To achieve this, cost tramway operators £21,943,147, but brought them in £27,262,361, yielding a profit of £5,319,214. Within three years passenger numbers had fallen by over 311 million, and they continued to do so year on year.

Above right:
By 1920, Edinburgh had the only major UK tramway that was not electrified. The Corporation took over control of the city's cable tramways on 1 July 1919. Despite a commitment to electrification, improvements were made to the ageing cable car stock. A number of cars, like No 185 here, were fitted with top covers. *IAL*

Right:
Edinburgh's cable trams gave sterling service to the end. Whilst a curious Tramways Department employee peers down, crowds of eager punters surge forward immediately so that the chain, complete with 'Musselburgh Races' sign, is removed from across the rear platform of a cable car. Conversion to electric traction was achieved remarkably quickly, and when the last cable car ran on 23 June 1923 it had been only one year and three days since the first electric tram had entered service. *IAL*

Right:
Wolverhampton's tramways were another late conversion to overhead electrification. In June 1920 it was decided to replace the original Lorain surface contact system and a conversion programme commenced. Newhampton Road East, shown above, formed part of route 2 to Whitmore Reans, and the first trams using this overhead ran on 28 August 1921. Destined for a short working life the last tram to Whitmore Reans ran on 1 October 1927. The service was replaced by motorbuses, but much of Wolverhampton's tramway system was converted to trolleybus operation, taking maximum advantage of the nearly new overhead power distribution equipment.
National Tramway Museum Collection

There were a number of reasons for the decline of tramways in the 1920s, including increased competition from bus and coach operators, and the growing popularity of the trolleybus. In addition, many tramway operators' powers, granted for 21 years under the Tramways Act — mostly in the 1900s — came up for renewal. Sometimes this coincided with an operator facing major expenditure for relaying worn track or replacing tramcars, so a number of them opted to abandon tramway operation in favour of an alternative form of public transport. Had they chosen to renew their operators' powers this would only have been granted for a further seven years before it had to be renewed again, another disincentive to continue tramway operation.

Great advances were made in motorbus design during the 1920s, through consultation and partnership between operators and vehicle manufacturers like AEC and Leyland. In 1920 a typical double-deck bus could seat 34, but by 1929 vehicles were being built that could, with various seating arrangements, seat 54 or 60. The development of large, high compression, high revolution, petrol engines, combined with general mechanical reliability, saw the production of buses that could carry a tram's load of passengers, whilst the needs of the latter were not overlooked either. Pneumatic tyres for large vehicles became available around 1925. Combined with efficient suspension and upholstered seating, these made a bus journey a far more inviting

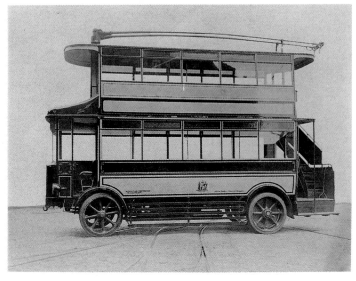

Above:
Competition and rivalry were keen between tram and bus operators in the 1920s, and situations sometimes became heated. This is probably a posed shot, possibly taken in November 1924 and intended to show how trams blocked the road for other users when they stopped. The driver of London General 'B'-type bus B1353 has incurred the wrath of a conductor on an anonymous London United Tramways car, and the latter is signalling back his displeasure in ritual semaphore. The bottom line on the football poster at left is exactly what many bus operators wanted to achieve. *IAL*

Left:
Birmingham Corporation Tramways Department trolleybus No 6 was one of 12 51-seater vehicles ordered in September 1921 to replace trams on route 7 to Nechells. The change was planned in response to the need to relay worn out track, but it gained greater significance as the first tramcar-to-trolleybus conversion ever undertaken in the UK. Trolleybuses took over the Nechells service on 27 November 1922, but the original vehicles had a relatively short working life, all being withdrawn in 1931/32. *Author's Collection*

prospect than a rough ride, seated on unforgiving wooden seats, aboard a tram travelling along worn and uneven tracks. Given a choice, the public voted with their — er — feet.

Another form of motorised transport to develop in this decade was the motor coach or charabanc. As with the motor haulage industry, a number of charabanc operators had their beginnings in war surplus chassis sold off by the War Ministry, mostly from a large vehicle dump at Slough. Although not generally direct competition to tram services, charabancs helped to change the image of public road transport to a service that went where people wanted, something that trackbound trams could not do.

Trolleybus development continued too, and history was made in Birmingham on 21 November 1922 when 12 double-deck Railless trolleybuses took over from trams on the two-mile Nechells route — the UK's first tram-to-trolleybus conversion. By 1929, 18 trolleybus systems had been constructed, the majority of which replaced tram routes. The number of trolleybus systems opening per year was:

1920	1	1925	4
1921	1	1926	2
1922	1	1927	3
1923	2	1928	3
1924	1	1929	0

Like motorbuses, the design of trolleybuses advanced, and the vehicles became lighter and larger, with pneumatic tyres. Great strides in the development of the trolleybus were made at Wolverhampton, where the need to install

Above:
From admittedly small beginnings, the amount of traffic on the roads increased considerably during the 1920s. One consequence of this was that traffic flows had to be controlled, and this photograph shows the traffic lights installed in Park Row, Leeds, in September 1928 for this purpose. For the tram heading towards the camera this was just the beginning of an ever increasing problem. *Modern Transport/IAL*

Below:
Wolverhampton Corporation trolleybus No 53 of 1928 shows just how far the design of these vehicles had come in a few years. The first trolleybus of this type entered service in Wolverhampton on 2 December 1926 and was the first six-wheeled, double-deck, covered-top trolleybus fitted with pneumatic tyres ever to be built. Wolverhampton converted its tramways to trolleybus operation in stages over seven years, commencing on 29 October 1923 and finishing on 27 October 1930. No 53 is seen in Victoria Square. *Author's Collection*

overhead wires in 1921, in place of the Lorain surface contact system, had produced a tramway with worn track and cars but an almost new power distribution system. Partly to maximise upon the latter, the Corporation had opted for trolleybuses after inspecting the Nechells route in nearby Birmingham. A programme of tram-to-trolleybus route conversions was set in place, starting on 23 July 1923 and taking until 27 January 1930 to complete.

The driving force behind the Wolverhampton programme was the transport department's General Manager & Engineer, Charles Owen Silvers, to whom must be credited a good deal of the innovation in trolleybus design during the interwar period. It was Silvers who hit upon the idea of capitalising on the advances made in motorbus design to produce trolleybuses that were lighter yet capable of carrying large passenger loads. By 1929 Wolverhampton had the largest trolleybus system in the world, and it was visited by many transport operators from the UK and overseas, including the Royal Commission on Transport then in session.

Under these forms of pressure, more and more tramway operators turned to motor and/or trolleybuses, and the number of electric tramway abandonments increasing yearly:

1920	0	1925	2
1921	2	1926	3
1922	0	1927	8
1923	0	1928	5
1924	1	1929	13

Above:
Another problem facing tramway operators in the 1920s was the age and condition of their rolling stock. This is a 'J' class car of the South Metropolitan Electric Tramways & Lighting Co Ltd (SMET). It was ordered for the opening of a route to Penge in June 1907, but by the early 1920s the class was showing body problems. Those slender window pillars were a weak point, and all had to be strengthened with angle irons, but a more radical solution was sought.
Modern Transport/IAL

Below:
Provincial traffic congestion was as nothing compared with the best that London could concoct. This is Whitechapel in the late 1920s, looking towards Aldgate. There are at least a dozen trams in view, including a Leyton Corporation car just entering the jam on the right, and an LCC car just escaping it on the left. Quite what those massive carts have on them is not clear, but the area was at the heart of the city's garment trade. *IAL*

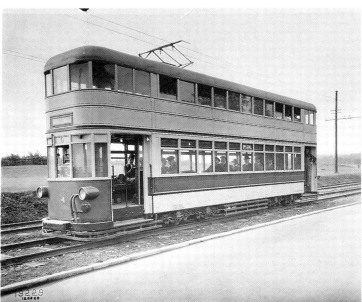

Above:
Early in 1928, SMET 'J' class car No 16 was rebuilt at the Metropolitan Electric Tramways' Hendon works, where it is seen. For added strength the lower saloon gained an extra window and pillar, and the body had flush sides formed from metal sheeting which extended up to replace the wire screens formerly used on the top deck. New upholstered seats were installed and the internal decoration was brightened up. The other 'J' class cars remaining in service were also rebuilt, but retained a four-window pattern on the saloon. Sadly, after all of this work and expense, the ex-SMET 'J' class cars were broken up by London Transport in 1935. *Modern Transport/IAL*

Left:
The UK's first passenger railway/tramway, the Swansea & Mumbles, was also its last to be electrified. Authorisation for this conversion was granted in May 1925, but the work took another four years. Away from the actual conversion work new rolling stock was also required. An order for 11 new tramcars was placed with the Brush Electrical Engineering Co of Loughborough in 1928. These were to have seats for 106 passengers and when designed and built became the largest trams to run anywhere in the UK. Car No 4 is seen on a proving trial shortly after delivery from Brush. *Modern Transport/IAL*

Left:
Brush's Swansea & Mumbles cars entered service on 2 March 1929. They were designed to be run in pairs, providing trains with a seating capacity of 216. The way that this was effected is shown in this makers' photograph, with connections for the braking and electrical systems in place. As the line ran along the coast, all the doors on these cars were located on the landward side. *Modern Transport/IAL*

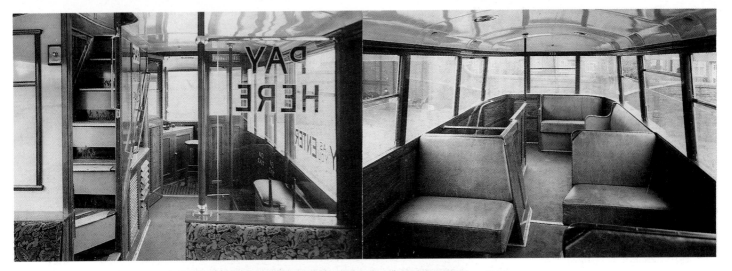

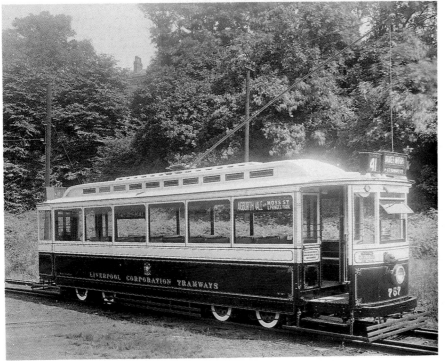

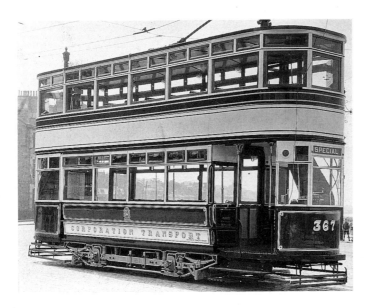

Above:
The levels of comfort and performance achieved by some motorbuses during the 1920s provided a stimulus to other tramway operators to retaliate. Modernising older cars brought some benefits, but a more modern design of tramcar was needed. This course of action was chosen by the Metropolitan Electric Tramways (MET) in 1926. Over the next three years a series of four experimental trams was built, the last two, by the Union Construction Company of Feltham (UCC). MET No 330 was the penultimate prototype for a class of 100 cars that would forever carry the name of their 'birthplace' — the Felthams. Illustrated are interior views of the lower and upper decks of MET 330, showing the high standard of comfort and finish. *Modern Transport/IAL*

Left:
Liverpool's commitment to tramways in the late 1920s was resolute, and its plans included the construction of a subway line to Everton. For this a new type of single-deck tramcar was proposed, one that could be coupled to others for multiple-unit operation. An order for a prototype car was placed with English Electric in June 1928. The finished tram, No 757, was based upon a design the company was then producing for Blackpool Corporation, known there as the 'Pantographs'. It is seen above on English Electric's test track before delivery to Liverpool on 23 July 1929. The car entered public service on 19 October 1929, but neither the subway idea nor the tramcar's design was continued. After just five years of service, No 757 was broken up in February 1935. *Liverpool Corporation*

Left:
For its first few years Edinburgh's newly-electrified tramway relied upon a mixture of converted cable cars, trams inherited from Leith Corporation and others built by outside suppliers. By the late 1920s the Corporation had a clearer idea of their requirements, and in 1929 they began to build a series of all-enclosed cars at their Shrubhill Works. No 367 was the first to be completed, in July 1929, the construction run continuing until 1931. *Modern Transport/IAL*

KEEPING THINGS GOING – TRAMWAY MAINTENANCE

Electric tramcars were noted for their resilience. Very rarely, perhaps only near to a car's withdrawal or at the end of tramway operation, did they appear in anything less than a good state of mechanical and physical repair. Systems varied of course, but many tramway operators took a pride in maintaining their tramcar fleet in a pristine condition. This meant a lot of hard work and investment on the operator's part; all ploughed into activities that took place largely in secret, in depots or special repair works, or at night. Many different skills were focused together in maintaining a tramway, and a great deal of specialist equipment was required. Special vehicles were also needed, as tramway maintenance involved the repair of the track and power distribution systems, every bit as much as it did the repairing of the trams themselves.

Small and large tramway systems differed with regard to the amount of maintenance they undertook themselves. This difference was partly a reflection of need: the operators of tramway systems with just a small number of trams and a few miles of track did not have the need for, or the means to provide, the major repair and overhaul facilities that larger tramways built for themselves. Instead, the former relied upon the multiple skills and dedication of small repair gangs, although some tramway companies that were subsidiaries of larger groups, such as the British Electric Traction Co Ltd, could benefit from the central purchasing of stores items, and make use of other repair facilities within the group.

Tramway maintenance was either planned or occasioned as the result of an accident or a failure of some part of the system. Depending upon the size of the tramway

Right:
Worcester's tram depot was in the Bull Ring, St John's, where the Worcester Electric Traction Co Ltd did most of its own repairs. Here, the motors from tramcar No 5 have recently been removed and the armatures are being tested. A subsidiary of the British Electric Traction Co, the Worcester company also made use of the BET's main repair works at Tividale in the Black Country.
National Tramway Museum Collection

Below right:
Many equipment manufacturers benefited from the boom in tramway building during the first decade or so of the 20th century — few more so than the crane makers, Herbert Morris & Co Ltd, of Loughborough. From a page in their 1912 catalogue one of Morris's travelling overhead cranes is seen lifting a motor in Birmingham Corporation Tramway's Main Repair Shop at its Kyotts Lake Road Works. *Author's Collection*

Below:
Morris's also made ancillary equipment for tramway operators, including this 'flat-jack for tramcars', seen being demonstrated on a Nottingham Corporation car. *Author's Collection*

H.M.B. FLAT-JACK FOR RAIL-CROSSINGS.

MAY BE LEFT UNDER THE RAIL WHILE TRAINS PASS OVER

PRICE EACH £5 10 0

SAFETY AND SMALL GANGS.

ELECTRIC OVERHEAD TRAVELLING-CRANES.

ASSEMBLERS, NOT MAKERS

undertaking, the majority of the items needed for its routine maintenance would be kept in store. This included asphalt, ballast, cement, overhead wire and fittings, rail, stone setts and traction poles, amongst hundreds of other essential items; plus the tools and equipment with which to install them. Other more unusual or specialist items, such as complicated pointwork, had to be bought-in, which, if required to repair some part of the system that was damaged unexpectedly, could be disruptive to the operation of the tramway and costly.

Routine maintenance of tramway systems would include such things as attention to the track, points and the overhead. Track wear, for example, was not uniform, and places where trams were required to brake often and sometimes harshly, wore away quicker than stretches where the system was more free-running. Ripples or corrugations often formed on the surface of rails where harsh braking was frequent, caused by the brakes locking tram wheels. These could be removed or reduced by grinding the rail

Below:
Temporary trackwork was installed for a variety of reasons. Here, at Croydon in 1923, car No 64 has just negotiated a passing loop laid in London Road, Norbury, while the other track of the Croydon Tramways was relayed for use by LCC trams, which were heavier than their Croydon counterparts. *IAL*

Bottom:
Liverpool Corporation Tramways opened a new tram works and depot at Edge Lane in October 1928. This had taken just over two years to complete. Below is the official photograph of the works and offices taken for the opening ceremony.
Harper & Taylor, Liverpool/Modern Transport/IAL

Opposite:
Part of the 'Press Pack' for the official opening of Liverpool Corporation's Edge Lane Works was this site plan, which details its layout and shows how repairs flowed through the building. The central traverser split the works in two: the left-hand side handling work associated with tramcar frames; the right-hand side that to do with their bodywork. A tram depot was also incorporated into the new complex; this can be seen at the extreme left. *Author's Collection*

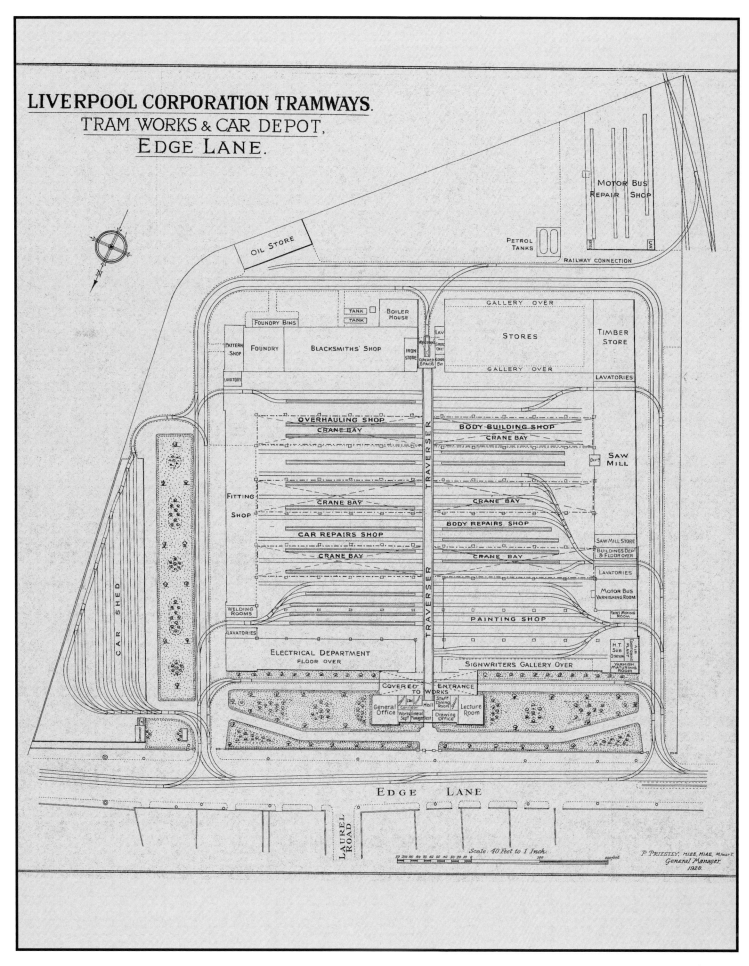

LIVERPOOL CORPORATION TRAMWAYS.
TRAM WORKS & CAR DEPOT,
EDGE LANE.

OIL STORE

MOTOR BUS REPAIR SHOP

PETROL TANKS

RAILWAY CONNECTION

FOUNDRY BINS

TANK
TANK

BOILER HOUSE

GALLERY OVER

STORES

TIMBER STORE

PATTERN SHOP

FOUNDRY

BLACKSMITHS' SHOP

IRON STORE

COVERED SPACE

GALLERY OVER

LAVATORIES

LAVATORY

OVERHAULING SHOP
CRANE BAY

BODY-BUILDING SHOP
CRANE BAY

SAW MILL

FITTING SHOP

CRANE BAY

CRANE BAY

TRAVERSER

CAR REPAIRS SHOP

BODY REPAIRS SHOP

SAW MILL STORE

BUILDINGS DEPT & FLOOR OVER

CRANE BAY

CRANE BAY

LAVATORIES

CAR SHED

TRAVERSER

MOTOR BUS VARNISHING ROOM

PAINT MIXING ROOM

WELDING ROOMS

PAINTING SHOP

LAVATORIES

H.T. SUB STATION

VARNISH MATURING ROOM

ELECTRICAL DEPARTMENT
FLOOR OVER

SIGNWRITERS GALLERY OVER

COVERED ENTRANCE TO WORKS

General Office

Works Supt

General Manager

Corridor

Hall

Staff Dining Room

Drawing Office

Lecture Room

EDGE LANE

LAUREL ROAD

Scale: 40 Feet to 1 Inch.

P. PRIESTLY. M.I.E.E. M.I.A.E. M.Inst.T.
General Manager.
1928.

surface, and larger tramways had rail grinding trams dedicated to this purpose. Points had to be kept free from road dirt and any items that might cause them to jam, and required frequent lubrication. Likewise, overhead wires had to kept clean and lubricated, special attention being paid to the 'frogs' or points where the overhead branched off. Extreme weather, such as heavy rain or snow, brought its own problems, and trams were fitted with snowploughs, or specially adapted trams — called snowbrooms — fitted with rotating brushes would be used to keep the tracks clear.

Systems with unusual features developed their own idiosyncratic maintenance regimes. Those using a surface contact method of power distribution had to pay especial attention to keeping the studs free from dirt or any items that might obstruct their movement, causing them to remain up and live. The LCC's conduit track presented unique problems. At three-quarters of an inch in width, the conduit slot was a handy size for all sorts of things to get stuck in it; these had to be removed. The channel beneath the slot was also a natural collecting point for water, and rain and road dirt combined to form a sludge that had to be removed regularly using special tankers.

Tramway services were also affected by other road works, major reconstructions or bridge repairs. These sometimes required the laying down of temporary tracks to divert tramway services around these obstructions. Some of these 'temporary diversions' lasted for a long time. For example, at Deptford Creek in London, a temporary bridge, erected to replace wartime bomb damage, remained in use until the withdrawal of tramway services.

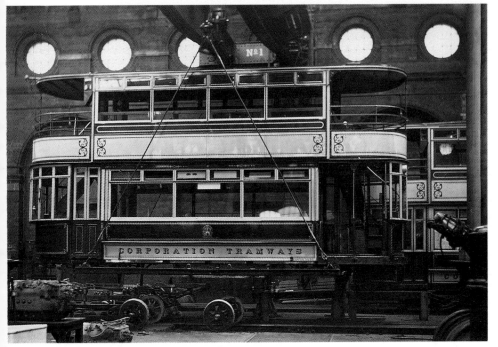

Above:
Edinburgh Corporation Tramways had an impressive repair and maintenance works at Shrubhill. Each tramcar was inspected thoroughly every six weeks, or every 5,000 miles or so. If an overhaul was deemed necessary the car would be driven to Shrubhill early one morning and would spend five to six days undergoing a complete inspection, clean and repair, including a repaint. Above, in a photograph taken around 1930, an Edinburgh tram is being washed before a thorough inspection, to determine whether a trip through Shrubhill was required. *IAL*

Left:
At Shrubhill Repair Works the freshly painted body of an Edinburgh tram is suspended from travelling crane No 1 ready to be dropped on to a reconditioned truck. The works overhauled an average of four trucks per week. *IAL*

Repairs to tramcars were generally undertaken at tram depots, but most city corporations who operated tramways built themselves large central repair works dedicated to this purpose. Illustrated earlier in this chapter is the Building & Repair Works that Liverpool Corporation built in Edge Lane for its Tramway & Motor Bus Undertaking in between 1926 and 1928. Opened in October 1928, Edge Lane Works comprised the following main sections:

- Electrical Shop — 23,670sq ft — for dealing with the repair and testing of all electrical equipment used on trams and buses;
- Car Repair Shop & Overhauling Shop — 87,750sq ft — equipped with 10 inspection pits and three overhead cranes for handling the routine maintenance of tramcars;
- Blacksmiths' Shop & Iron Store — 9,900sq ft — containing 15 hearths and used for the maintenance of tramcar frames;
- Pattern Shop — 1,670sq ft — for producing patterns for the Foundry;
- Foundry — 3,620sq ft — with 12 furnaces, to provide castings for use in bearings, controllers, circuit breakers, overhead, sign fittings, trolley heads, etc, in brass and aluminium;
- Painters' Shop — 32,210sq ft — with facilities for painting, coachlining and signwriting, and a maximum capacity of 40 trams at any one time;
- Body Repair Shop — 41,400sq ft — with a maximum capacity of 30 trams;
- Body Building Shop — 24,048sq ft — including a saw mill, this shop could hold 24 trams at any one time;
- Stores — 20,898sq ft — for the holding of spare parts;
- Timber Stores — 22,764sq ft — a three-storey building for seasoning timber.

Top:
The rarely seen practice of weighing a tramcar. Edinburgh No 260 was a new all-metal construction car made for the Corporation by Metropolitan Cammell and delivered in 1932. The box above the cradle beam is a weighing scale, and this shiny new tram tipped these at a little over 12 tons. *IAL*

Above:
Few tramways had facilities to match London Transport's Central Car Repair Depot at Charlton in southeast London. Built by the former LCC Tramways, the first section of the works opened on 5 March 1909. Around 1934, the body of ex-LCC 'E/1' class tramcar No 1773 is seen being hoisted off its bogies in preparation for an overhaul. *V. C. Jones Collection/IAL*

Left:
Edinburgh car No 264 is undergoing a tilt test at the Corporation's Shrubhill Repair Works. This tested the tram's centre of gravity. Weighing 9 tons 9cwt, the centre of gravity was just under 5ft from rail level, permitting a tilt of 25° from the vertical before the car fell over. According to the scale at left, there's a degree or so to go yet. *IAL*

Above:
Not all tramway repair and maintenance work was planned. On 29 November 1920, Dudley-Stourbridge car No 77 was descending Castle Hill, Dudley, when it skidded on greasy rails and careered down the gradient at up to 40mph. Leaving the rails by Dudley Opera House, it hit a cart, mounted the pavement, and came to a halt with its front third hanging over a bridge above Dudley station — a 60ft drop. Seen here from the top of a tram held up by the accident; the driver, conductor and all 14 passengers escaped the crash with shock, but something made the first helpers on the scene think that the accident was much more serious — the struck cart had been loaded with bones! *Author*

Left:
Bridge widening work in Commonside West, Mitcham Common, required the installation of temporary tram track to maintain the service. On 4 October 1936 ex-LCC Class E car No 436 is just crowning the bridge as part of its journey on route 30. Movement over the bridge was controlled by a signalman who operated a simple 'Stop-Go' board, seen protruding from the roof of a temporary pointsman's cabin. Within a year the tram would be withdrawn and its route replaced by trolleybus route 630, on 12 September 1937.
H. F. Wheeler Collection/Roger Carpenter

The majority of tramway operators undertook a programme of maintenance for their tramcar fleet under which each car received regular attention. The following practice is an amalgam, based upon the inspection routines followed by a number of tramways:

DAILY — INSPECT:
- bells, pushes and batteries;
- bodywork;
- lamps and switches;
- lifeguards;
- sand hoppers, top up as required;
- trolley heads, wheels, contacts;
- trucks, and clean car inside and out.

TWICE-WEEKLY — INSPECT:
- controllers, clean and lubricate contacts.

WEEKLY — INSPECT:
- Commutators, brush holders and brushes in the motors;
- Lubricate axle bearings.

FORTNIGHTLY — INSPECT:
- Armature bearings in the motors, and lubricate these.

MONTHLY — INSPECT:
- Armature clearances.

Less frequently a tramcar would undergo a thorough overhaul, passing through the following stages:

- Body lifting — to enable the truck/bogies to be removed;
- Truck/bogie replacement — with reconditioned units;
- Inspection — of the the body, electrical items, glazing, upholstery, etc;
- Replacement of the controllers, trolley-bases, trolley poles and trolley heads with reconditioned units;
- Paintshop — for the body to be painted and varnished;
- Drying area — for the paint/varnish to 'go-off';
- A test run.

Below:
Older passenger cars were often converted for works' duties after withdrawal from revenue service. This Aberdeen tram appears to have an identity crisis as it is No 23 on the front and No 58 on the side. The car had already enjoyed quite a history, having been built as a horse tram and converted, as one of a batch of 13 such cars, to electric traction in 1900-3. *The late W. A. Camwell*

Bottom:
Tramway maintenance involved the use of a number of specialised vehicles. One of the most general of these, seen on many tramway systems, was a stores or tool van, the purpose of which was to transport spares and equipment in between depots and around a tramway system. Aberdeen Corporation Tramways built their own tram especially for this purpose in 1902. *The late W. A. Camwell*

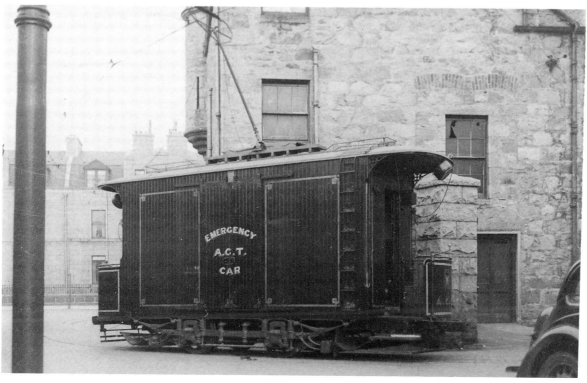

Right:
The LPTB also converted older classes of tramcars to works cars. No 015 was used as a sand carrier and is seen ferrying this important material between depots around the system in April 1948. It had begun life as a double-decker — LCC Class C car No 273 — and had been withdrawn following delivery of new Class HR/2 cars in 1931. Eighteen others of the 'C' class were converted for use as snowploughs, which gives some indication of the numbers of specialist vehicles needed to keep a large tramway system going.
V. C. Jones Collection/IAL

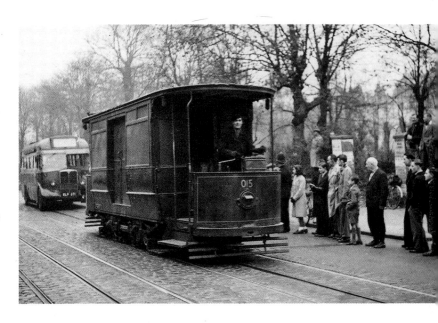

Below:
Upon the formation of the London Passenger Transport Board (LPTB) and 'London Transport' on 1 July 1933 the new body acquired tram depots and repair facilities from other tramway operators. Croydon Tramways' main repair facility was provided at its Thornton Heath depot, where four cars are seen standing over inspection pits. Nos 1002 and 1417 were ex-LCC Class E/1 cars, whilst No 375, and the anonymous tram on the right, were both ex-Croydon cars, the latter being one of four such trams to be improved under the LPTB's rehabilitation programme in November and December 1936.
Modern Transport/IAL

Above:
Repair work sometimes came a little too close to home. On 11 April 1948, 22 tramcars were damaged or destroyed in a fire at Newlands depot in Glasgow. This shows the site of the fire less than a month afterwards, before reconstruction work had begun. Newlands closed as a tram depot on 21 October 1961. *The late Michael Waller/Peter Waller*

Left:
On smaller tramway systems works' cars were sometimes multi-purpose. Bury No 1 doubled as both a stores van and snowplough and is seen at 5pm on 9 October 1948, just four months before the closure of Bury's tramways.
The late Michael Waller/Peter Waller

Opposite above:
Another tramway system to make good use of older classes of passenger tramcars as works' cars was Blackpool. Overhead line car No 4 (later No 754) was rebuilt in 1934 from No 31, one of a class of trams known as the 'Marton Box Cars', originally built in 1901. Seen at Thornton Gate on 18 April 1949, the car, equipped with an elevating platform, was used mainly for painting traction poles and maintaining the overhead wires. Blackpool No 4's subsequent history also serves to highlight the benefit that the common tramway practice of recycling older cars for works' duties has had for future generations. The car retired from its duties in Blackpool in April 1983 and was moved to the open-air industrial museum at Beamish in July 1984. Four years later, in May 1988, she re-emerged as 'Marton Box Car' No 31, and sees regular service on the tramway at Beamish. *The late Michael Waller/Peter Waller*

Opposite below:
Although the programme to replace London's trams — christened 'Operation Tramaway' — was not announced until 5 July 1950, it had been in the planning stage since 1948. It was against this background that the newly-created London Transport Executive (LTE) undertook the decision to lay two new sections of conduit track. The first was over a temporary lifting bridge at Deptford Creek and was required to maintain route 70. This was laid during the spring of 1949, and is seen above nearing completion. *IAL*

Above:
One could be mistaken for thinking that this photograph shows a scene on a Belgian or German tramway — but it does not. The city is Leeds and the date is some time in the late 1940s (note the blackout paint on the tree at left). Leading is railgrinder No 2, followed by works' car No 6, a converted ex-Hull passenger car, and what is probably works car No 1. The reason for this concentration of attention is unknown. *Robert F. Mack*

Right:
The new track at Deptford Creek came into use during July 1949, and 'E/1' class cars Nos 586 and 552 are seen easing their way through the still uncompleted works. Trams continued to use this temporary trackwork for another year, until the last cars ran on route 70 on 10 July 1951. *IAL*

Above:
Well into its 'Operation Tramaway' programme the LTE was required to reroute the conduit track at the junction of Westminster Bridge, Lambeth Palace and York roads, as part of the preparations for the Festival of Britain. The work was undertaken to remove a bottleneck at the junction, where serious traffic jams formed at peak times. Work began early in 1950, and here curves are being laid from Addington Street into a 'New Street', formed to give access to Westminster Bridge Road. *V. C. Jones Collection/IAL*

Right:
More public than the Deptford Creek trackwork, the Westminster scheme gave the first opportunity for a generation or more to study the laying of conduit track. This close-up of the Addington Street/New Street pointwork shows both its basic construction and way that the trackwork — supplied by Hadfields of Sheffield — was carefully labelled. Trams first ran on these rails on 11 June 1950, and the whole scheme was completed by that December. The pace of tramway abandonment meant that some of these new lines saw little use, one section being used only for 11 weeks! *V. C. Jones Collection/IAL*

Right:
At Windsor Street, Dundee on 20 April 1951, the photographer's shadow is caught recording the relaying of a reverse curve. The setts piled up on the left would be relaid when the work was completed. Expertly maintained to the end, Dundee's last tram ran on 21 October 1956.
The late Michael Waller/Peter Waller

Below:
Few tramway systems were better maintained than Dundee's. The decision to abandon the tramway was taken quite late in its working life, and track relaying was undertaken widely in the early 1950s. In Murraygate on 16 September 1950, tram lines are exposed as part of a general road reconstruction.
The late Michael Waller/Peter Waller

10

ELECTRIC TRAMS TO 1939

The 1930s would see the greatest number of tramway abandonments and tram-to-trolleybus conversions in the UK of any decade in the 20th century. All the factors and pressures outlined earlier continued to exert their influence upon these decisions. A policy of tramway abandonment also received official sanction with the publication of the final report of the Royal Commission on Transport in December 1930. Chapter five of the report considered 'Tramways and Trackless Trolley Vehicles', and concluded that the tram: '...possesses certain disadvantages so serious that we think it probable that had the motor omnibus been invented at the time when tramways were first authorised not a single mile of tramway would ever have been laid down.'

Spelling these out the Royal Commission recorded that trams:

■ 'constitute most grievous obstructions to all other forms of road traffic';
■ and that: 'when motor omnibuses run on the same routes the congestion in many places becomes intolerable'.
■ It also stated that: 'tramlines in wet weather are often a cause of skidding both to motor cars and cycles';
■ and that: 'the fact that a tramcar cannot be steered involves a greater liability to collisions than is the case with other vehicles'.

Concluding, in paragraph 372, the Royal Commission recommended:

■ a) that no additional tramways should be constructed;
■ b) that, though no definite time limit can be laid down, they should gradually disappear and give place to other forms of transport.

Of trolleybuses, the Royal Commission noted that they had: 'the advantage of visiting Wolverhampton, where ... a trackless trolley system appears to give excellent results.' This notwithstanding, they came down firmly in favour of the motorbus.

Below:
The final prototype Feltham car was MET No 331, completed by the UCC Co in June 1930. Outwardly similar to the production 'Felthams' that would follow, No 331's most obvious difference was its central entrance doors. These were air-operated and led to a lowered central vestibule off which was a pair of staircases. Designed as an experiment in Pay-As-You-Enter fare collection, the conductor was supposed to stay in the vestibule and dispense tickets from a fixed position ticket machine. MET No 331 became LPTB No 2168 but was withdrawn from service in 1936, being sold on to Sunderland in January 1937 where she became No 100. Only used fitfully there, the car was stored during World War 2 and taken out of service in May 1951. Bought by the LRTL in 1952, No 331 was stored at West Auckland and Bradford before going to Crich in mid-1961 where, after many years in storage, she has been restored. *Modern Transport/IAL*

Whereas, two decades previously, there had been a mania to build and/or electrify tramways, there was now a mania to get rid of them. And, in a similar way to how some tramways had been built where they were not really needed, in this new purging zeal lines were closed where they should have been kept open. One such casualty, just nine years and two months after it had opened, was the Dearne & District Light Railways, which closed on 30 September 1933.

Motorbus design took a major step forward with the adoption of diesel (or 'oil' as it was known at that time) engines. This fuel was cheaper to produce, and thus to buy, and diesel-engined buses did more miles to the gallon than an equivalent vehicle running on petrol. From trials in London and Sheffield in 1930, the use of diesel-engined buses spread throughout the country in between 1933 and 1937, so much so that by 1939, 65% of London Transport's 5,000+ buses were diesel-powered. Designers also found that, combined with new forms of transmission, diesel engines could be placed in positions other than at the front of a bus, thereby eliminating the need for the 'snout' so characteristic of early buses.

Trolleybus design continued to develop, with a move towards lightweight bodies using an all-metal construction. Twenty new trolleybus systems opened during the 1930s, each being a replacement for a tramway. The number of new trolleybus systems opening each year was:

1930	2	1935	1
1931	3	1936	2
1932	3	1937	2
1933	2	1938	2
1934	2	1939	1

Not all tramways buckled under these onslaughts. Even the damning Royal Commission on Transport had agreed with witnesses that: *'where they are kept up-to-date, tramways are very efficient; that in London and other big urban areas where heavy traffic has to be dealt with tramcars are superior to any other form of road passenger vehicles and could not economically be replaced by omnibuses or trackless trolley vehicles'*. Transport operators in those 'big urban areas' tended to agree with this view and, in the big cities especially, rather than scrap their tramways councils invested in them:

- Lines were built to serve new housing developments, linking suburban housing directly to city centres and places of work. Liverpool's proud boast during the 1930s was that it had built one new tramway line to serve one new housing development each year.
- Addressing the criticism of trams obstructing other road traffic a number of local authorities took the opportunity afforded by road improvements to relocate tramlines into central reservations, away from other traffic. As a result, trams could operate at higher speeds and other road users were not impeded.
- Contemporary bus designs provided greater levels of passenger comfort than most trams and so advantage was taken of advances in motor body construction to produce lightweight trams with all-metal bodies. New technology included air brakes and air-operated doors, drivers' cabins and seats, and for their passengers these trams now had upholstered seats and heaters.

For those with a love of trams the 1930s was a frustrating time. One man, Jay William Fowler, was determined to do something to redress the balance of opinion against tramways. Fowler was a printer by trade, with a family printing business in Cricklewood. Together with some colleagues he formed an informal alliance, tentatively called the Light Railway Transport League (LRTL), late in 1936. Internal ructions racked the group, and matters came to a head at a meeting held on 24 November 1937. Fowler triumphed and the LRTL was put on a sound footing. It existed to advocate tramways, with the aim of: *'securing for every suitable area the comfortable, cheap and safe light railway transport which modern developments have made possible'*. The LRTL published a monthly journal, *The Modern Tramway*, and organised tours of tramway systems in the UK and abroad. Over the years, the LRTL, now the Light Rail Transit Association (LRTA) has amassed a detailed collection of information and photographs on tramways. Those who came to an interest in trams after they had mostly disappeared from the UK's streets will be forever in the debt of Jay Fowler and the LRTL.

Sadly, despite these positive moves, 81 tramway undertakings were abandoned during the 1930s, the number of closures per year being:

1930	10	1935	8
1931	14	1936	7
1932	9	1937	9
1933	9	1938	1
1934	8	1939	6

Below:
Anyone who had been far away from Manchester for almost 50 years could be forgiven for not realising that the city had been without trams for most of that time. On 23 September 1931 an aerial photographer managed to capture 14 trams in this view over Piccadilly looking along Market Street. Once the hub of the Manchester tramway system, Metrolink trams now ply their way through much of this area, renamed Piccadilly Gardens. *Aerofilms*

Above:

Investment was poured into a number of large town and city tramway systems during the 1930s, but for many others the decade brought just one thing — closure. The end of the line came for the Mansfield & District Light Railway Co on 9 October 1932. This line-up, right-to-left, shows car No 6, one of the original fleet that opened the tramway on 11 July 1905, either car No 27 or No 28, the only totally-enclosed trams in the fleet, and one of the replacement motorbuses. Few photographs could emphasise better the advances made in bus design through the 1920s. Although only seven years separate the bus and the tram next to it, they could almost be from different centuries. The bus is so shiny that there appears to be a third member of the crew standing by it. Tramcars Nos 27 and 28 were sold to Sunderland where they were rebuilt. *IAL*

Right:

Closure came to the Dewsbury, Ossett & Soothill Nether Tramways on 19 October 1933, after 25 years' service. The service was provided by the National Electric Construction Co on behalf of the three local authorities named. On the left is car No 7 and on the right car No 11, both seen outside Martins Bank at the Dewsbury terminus. Car No 11 was a low-height tram bought from the Mexborough & Swinton Tramways in 1928. *Walter Gratwicke*

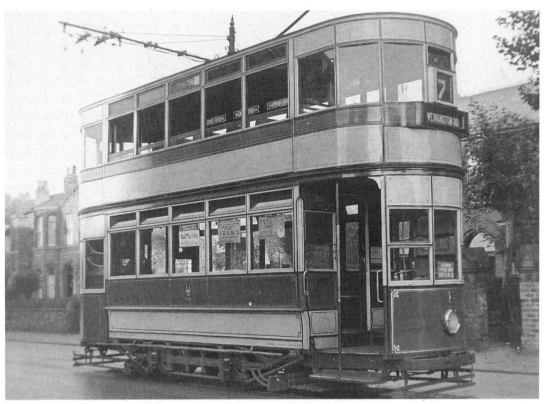

Opposite above:
Electric trams first ran in Southport on 18 July 1900. In 1913 the Corporation obtained an Act permitting the use of trolleybuses, but let the powers lapse, one to use motorbuses in 1921, and a further Act relating to the use of trolleybuses in 1930. Until 31 December 1917 the tramways were operated by the Southport Tramways Co, but the Corporation purchased this undertaking with effect from the following day. The system was nine route miles and worked by 36 trams. Abandonment in favour of motorbuses took place in stages from 1931 until final closure on 31 December 1934. Car No 1 is seen in 1933 on the Wennington Road route 7. *IAL*

Opposite below:
In 1933 the transport trade press was full of the advances made in the production of all-metal bus bodies. Edinburgh Corporation was keen to see how this technology would work with tramcars and took delivery of examples produced by Metropolitan-Cammell and Hurst Nelson. The latter supplied three cars in September 1934 — Nos 231, 239 and 240 — one of which is seen here turning into Stanley Road from Craighall

Road. Someone clearly disliked the idea that one of Edinburgh's new trams might be thought to have a chimney sticking out of its roof, and so they doctored this photograph to remove it (see inset). Edinburgh Corporation finally selected a tramcar design incorporating aluminium alloy castings, aluminium sheets and plywood, taking delivery of 84 such trams in the years to 1950. *Scottish Pictorial Press/Modern Transport/IAL*

Above:
Upon its formation on 1 July 1933 the London Passenger Transport Board (LPTB) acquired the assets of 14 separate tramway undertakings, including 2,630 trams and 328 route miles of tramway. Melding these into a coherent, corporate unit took some time. A decision about a standard livery was not announced until May 1934 from when, as overhauls proceeded, this was applied. By far the greatest number of trams came from the former LCC Tramways and here ex-LCC 'HR/2' class car No 155 is seen soon after acquiring the new livery. No 155 was one of a batch of 58 cars built for use solely within the confines of the LCC's conduit system; as a result of this, none of the batch was fitted with trolley poles. *LTE*

Above:
One of the larger provincial tramways to be abandoned during the 1930s was Nottingham Corporation's, the first section of which opened on 1 January 1901. At its greatest extent the system had 12 routes, covering 25 route miles, and a fleet of 200 well-maintained trams. Closure was progressive, protracted and mostly in favour of trolleybuses, starting with the Nottingham Road route on 9 April 1927 and ending with the Sherwood route and Arnold extension on 5 September 1936. Car No 192 of 1926/27 is seen at Colwick Crossing, the terminus of route D, sometime after 1933, when route letters were adopted, and before 1 June 1935, when the route was abandoned. After closure of the system, No 192 was sold to Aberdeen Corporation.
G. H. F. Atkins

Opposite above:
As the LPTB undertook further integration of the varied transport undertakings it had inherited upon formation, some of the older classes

of tramcars were scrapped. South Metropolitan Electric Tramways & Lighting Co Ltd (SMET) car No 40s was one of 52 similar cars that was not renumbered into the main LPTB fleet — hence the suffix letter. It is seen on ex-SMET route 5 to Crystal Palace on 6 July 1935. Seven months later, on 9 February 1936, trolleybuses replaced trams on this route and the trams were withdrawn from service and broken up.
H. F. Wheeler Collection/R. S. Carpenter

Opposite below:
Belfast Corporation went to great lengths to integrate tram and railway services; at both Queen's Quay and York Road stations cars ran into special bays inside the station buildings. 'Standard Red' car No 2, seen here emerging from the bay at York Road station, was one of the original vehicles that inaugurated electric tramcar services in Belfast on 29 November 1905. *Author's Collection*

Above:
Like Edinburgh, Belfast Corporation also invested in new lightweight tramcars during the 1930s. Designs were produced by the Transport Department's General Manager & Engineer, Col. R. McCreary, in 1935. The contract to produce the cars was split between English Electric in Preston and a local firm, the Service Motor Works. Fifty of these 'McCreary' cars, as they became known, were made; No 427 was one of the English Electric cars and is seen here on the Queen's Road route. *IAL*

Opposite:
This photograph was taken in September 1935 to show an AEC 'Q'-type bus in service in Aberdeen. The 'Qs' were diesel-engined and the first production buses to have their engines anywhere other than at the front — it was positioned under the body, behind the front wheel. Body styles varied; this version seated 39 and was rear entrance-exit. Strikingly modern against the Aberdeen Corporation tramcars also caught in this frame, the city's trams had a week or two left in them yet, the last car running on 3 May 1958. *Modern Transport/IAL*

Below:
Another problem faced by the infant LPTB was a profusion of tram depots — 35 of them in all. Holloway Depot above, was well-equipped. This is just one of its three traversers. Around the time that this photograph was taken, c1936, the depot was converted for dual use by trolleybuses. Its principal tramcar holding was cars for the three Kingsway Subway services, routes 31, 33, and 35. Sitting in track 24 is one of the original single-decked subway cars, withdrawn in 1930 and not officially part of the LPTB fleet. The holes beneath the tracks are for the conduit ploughs, which seem to have been slewed over to alongside one of the running rails. *LTE*

Opposite:
Liverpool's most modern tramcars were its streamlined bogie cars. Designed and built by the Corporation at its Edge Lane Works these used a mixture of modern and traditional construction methods. An oak and ash body frame was constructed upon a steel underframe, the exterior being panelled in aluminium. The first car completed was No 868, in June 1936, and it is seen here on a reserved section of route 8. Edge Lane turned these cars out at the rate of three a week and had built total of 163 'Green Goddesses', as they were nicknamed, by the end of 1937. The next car, No 869, was one of 46 sold to Glasgow Corporation in 1953 and 1954. After serving as Glasgow No 1055, the car was acquired by the Merseyside Tramway Preservation Society. Subsequently restored as a Liverpool car, No 869 is amongst the collection of tramcars at the National Tramway Museum at Crich. *Modern Transport/IAL*

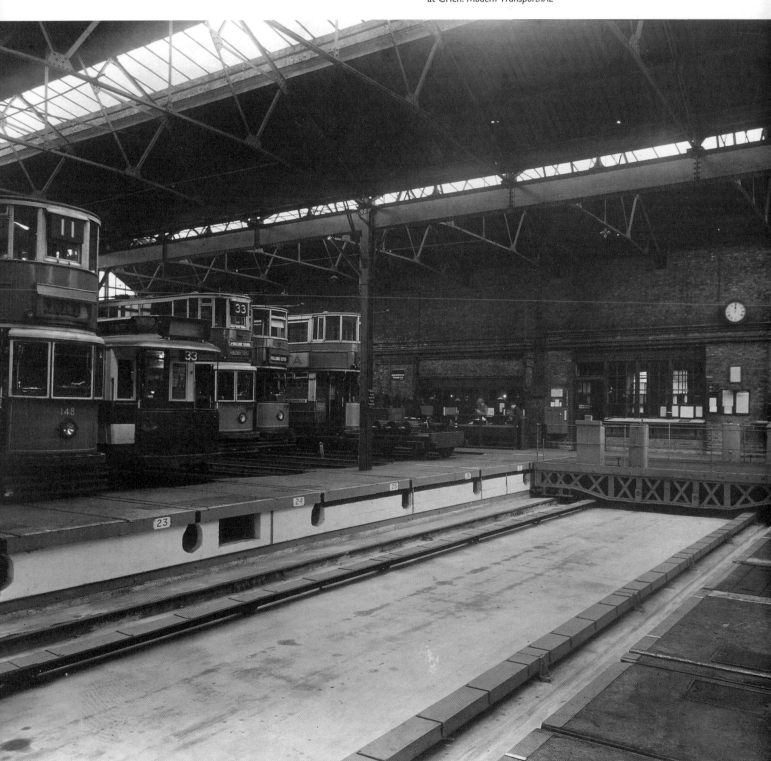

Above:
The LPTB also thinned-out its fleet of trams inherited from the larger former tramway operators. No 2237 was an ex-MET 'H' class car of c1912. It is seen in the rain on 26 December 1935 at the city terminus of route 19 to Barnet, by the Tottenham Court Road-Hampstead Road junction. The route was withdrawn on 6 March 1938, and No 2237 remained in service for another eight months before being scrapped.
H. F. Wheeler
Collection/R. S. Carpenter

Right:
An early application form for the Light Railway Transport League (LRTL): founded in 1937, the LRTL declared itself 'pro tram' and concerned itself 'with advocating tramways and other light railways under suitable conditions'. In almost 70 years the League, now the Light Rail Transit Association (LRTA), has built up a detailed collection of information and photographs on tramways, as well as considerable expertise on the subject.

MEMBERSHIP AND/OR MAGAZINE SUBSCRIPTION
SOLICITED

FOR OFFICE USE ONLY.

Ref. No.   Roll.   Rec.
Card.   Area.   M.T.
Badge.   Sec.

LIGHT RAILWAY TRANSPORT LEAGUE.

To Mr. J. W. FOWLER, *Hon. Treasurer, 245, Cricklewood Broadway, London, N.W.2.*

*I should like to become a member of the Light Railway Transport League, for which I enclose 5/- as my annual subscription, dating from date given below.

*Please send me one broach/stud type badge, 1/6 (plus 3d. postage and packing if no other communication).

*Please ask the Editor to include my name on the mailing list for future copies of " The Modern Tramway," for which I enclose...................................in advance payment of...................copies each issue and for this issue, at the rate of 4d. per copy, post free (annual subscription 4/-).

*Please send a specimen copy to...
mentioning my name.

My chief interest is...
(e.g., Correspondence with others of similar interest in Great Britain—Abroad; General; Historical; Modelling; Modernisation; Photography; Retention and Extension of Tramways; Technical; Visits to various systems.)

*CROSS OUT LINES THAT DO NOT APPLY.

Signed..

Address..
.... Date.........................

13391 FL.

11
DOING THEIR BIT – TRAMS AT WAR

rams played an important role in the two world wars of the 20th century, although their circumstances were markedly different in each conflict. World War 1 came at a time when electric tramways proliferated throughout the country, and many were still expanding to meet the needs of suburban populations. Such developments were mostly deferred by the demands of war, unless any new lines were to serve factories engaged in vital munitions or aircraft work. New services were introduced to meet the needs of these factories, many of which adopted the three-shift 24hr working day — the first time this was seen in the UK. The induction of thousands upon thousands of men into the forces also left its mark on tramway operation, as women took the places of tram conductors. In marked contrast to World War 2, there was little direct damage to those living and working on the Home Front, although in some areas bombing raids from Zeppelins were a feature of the later part of the war.

By 1939 much had changed. Tramways were on the decline in the UK, and more routes were being closed than opened. German air raids, particularly in the first half of the war, did massive damage to towns and cities up and down the country, disrupting tramway operation and worsening an already acute shortage of materials with which to effect repairs. Directly, World War 2 caused the closure of only two tramways, in Coventry and Bristol. Both systems had embarked upon programmes of replacing trams with buses around 1936, and were left with just three and four tram routes respectively. The track, overhead and power supply to Coventry's tramways were devastated during the massive air raid of 14/15 November 1940 — the trams did not run again — although most of the cars themselves escaped damage. In Bristol, one pair of routes was forcibly withdrawn after a direct hit on Bedminster depot on 3 January 1941 that destroyed most of the cars inside. Four months later, at around 10pm on 11 April 1941, the power supply to the remaining routes was severed in another air raid, ending 45 years of tramway operation in Bristol at a stroke.

Right above:
Women were recruited as tram conductors during World War 1, and as tram drivers during World War 2. Southampton Corporation took a lead in this, establishing a training programme for lady conductors early in 1942. Pictured is Mrs S. L. Staples, one of the first four women to qualify as tram drivers under this scheme. Mrs Staples' father had been a tram driver with the Corporation for over 20 years; his daughter is pictured at the controls of car No 94 on 3 April 1942.
Topical Press Agency

Right:
Halifax Corporation was very inventive in its use of trams during World War 1. Here a car has been dressed up in a very patriotic manner to put across the message that 'YOUR COUNTRY NEEDS YOU FOR THE WEST RIDING REGIMENT' to the young men of the area.
National Tramway Museum Collection

Top right:
By the middle of World War 2 supplies of spare parts to keep trams and trolleybuses going were drying up. A number of transport undertakings began to reclaim parts through the use of nickel and chromium electro-deposition, and oxy-acetylene and electric welding. This display was mounted by the LPTB in May 1943 to show the strides it had made in Tram & Trolleybus Reclamation Work. Pictured are various components recovered using the processes mentioned; these include trolleybus stub axles and tramcar bogie parts and bearing housings. *Topical Press Agency*

Right:
More inventive still of Halifax Corporation was this Kitchen Car, built to serve the culinary needs of war workers. The car is seen at Skircoat Road depot in 1916 with a limited but appetising menu and a schedule of the locations it would be visiting. *National Tramway Museum Collection*

Below:
Dramatic evidence of the damage caused to tramways by air raids during World War 2. Although the main casualty was a bus (LT669), the conduit tramlines had also been severed. This was the scene in Balham High Road on the morning of 7 November 1940 following an air raid. Tram services were partially resumed on 20 November, but the bus remained in the crater for over two weeks. Concern was so high over the effect on morale of publishing this photograph that it was embargoed for almost two years, not being passed by the censor until 23 January 1942. *Fox Photos*

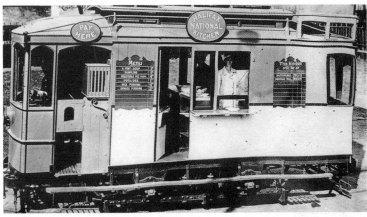

12

DECORATED TRAMS – FINALE AND EXIT

Events surrounding the abandonment of electric tramway operation ran the entire gamut, from the perfunctory act of simply not running any trams the following day, to raising one of the mightiest hoo-haas many places had seen in years. Last tram ceremonies were also the final opportunity tramway operators had to prepare decorated trams — and some did it in style.

Below:
For the sake of five days, Hull Corporation Tramways could have celebrated both the abandonment of tramcar operation and its 46th anniversary on the same day. Opened on 5 July 1899, the end came on 30 June 1945 and for the occasion this special decorated car was prepared, replete with flags, bunting and light bulbs spelling out the Corporation tramway department's initials and the years of operation. As Hull's tramway was wound down a number of tramcars were sold on to Leeds, where the last ex-Hull tram of all ran in 1955. *IAL*

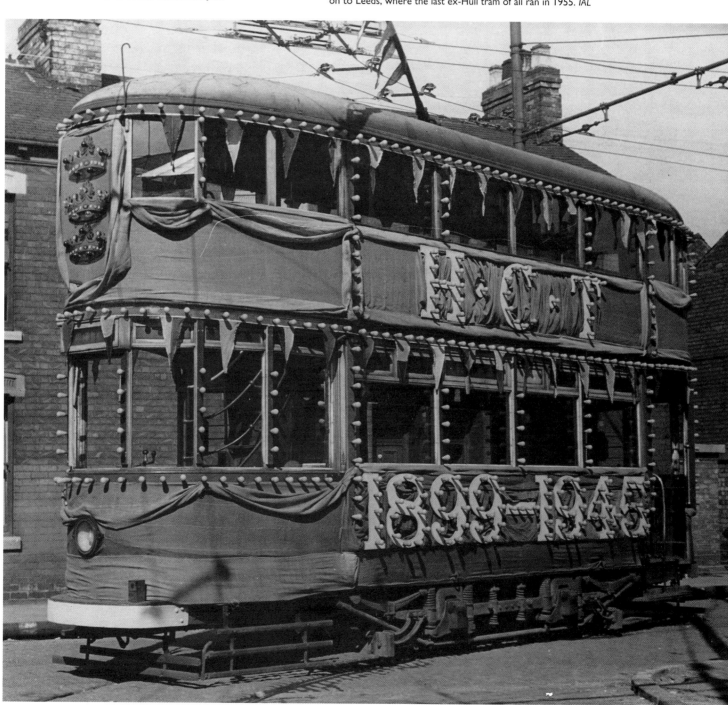

Right:
In contrast, Sunderland's Official Last Tram, No 86, had one of the shortest farewell slogans of any tramway abandonment: 'Retiring October 1st 1954'. On that day it brought up the rear of a special convoy of nine tramcars that ran from Sunderland Town Hall to Seaburn and back to Wheat Sheaf depot. Seen receiving last-minute attention outside the latter, No 86 was to serve the Sunderland populous one more time when, on 29 October 1954, it was towed out of the depot and used as a grandstand for retired transport department employees to see HM The Queen on a visit to the city. *Sunderland Echo*

Below:
A father lifts his daughter up for a better view of Cardiff's last tramcar. Opened on 2 May 1902, the last service trams ran on 19 February 1950, but the following day this elaborately-lit and adorned tramcar was run alongside its replacement trolleybuses on the Whitchurch Road route 1. Cardiff's last tram carried possibly the longest farewell slogan of all, taking the form of a personal message from the tramcar extolling the years of service it had given to the citizens of the city. *R. W. A. Jones/Author's Collection*

ELECTRIC TRAMS FROM 1945

Much as World War 1 had halted tramway development, World War 2 halted tramway abandonment. Those towns and cities that still had working tramway systems on 8 May 1945 included a number that, but for the war, would have replaced their trams with buses or trolleybuses in the early 1940s. London was amongst that number, and a programme of tramway replacement planned for those years was delayed for a decade as a result of the war and the austerity period that followed. Indeed, in London's abandonment proposals, substituting the year 1950 for 1940, and so on, gives a very accurate picture of the programme that was eventually followed.

Many tramways were living on borrowed time, and some did not wait long to complete their closure proposals. The first postwar tramway abandonment was by Hull Corporation on 30 June 1945. Hull had sold a number of trams to Leeds Corporation in 1942, and upon the closure of its system, it sold some more to the same city. This set a trend for a trade in second-hand trams that continued until 1954. In summary, (excluding second-hand cars acquired before 1939) the tramcar acquisitions made during this period were:

- Aberdeen: 14 Manchester trams;
- Edinburgh: 11 Manchester trams;
- Gateshead: six Oldham trams, five Newcastle trams;
- Glasgow: 46 Liverpool trams;
- Grimsby & Immingham Railway: three Newcastle trams, 18 Gateshead trams;
- Leeds: 43 Hull trams, 91 London trams, seven Manchester trams, 22 Southampton trams, one Sunderland tram;
- Llandudno: two Darwen trams;
- Sunderland: one South Shields tram, one Bury tram, six Manchester trams.

Right:
Manchester's last service trams were supposed to run on 9 January 1949, with a ceremonial procession the following morning. Four trams, Nos 113, 976, 978 and 1007, had been specially cleaned to take part in this event, but come the morning there weren't enough buses to cope with the rush-hour, so all four cars, plus reserve No 102, were pressed into service. The procession formed up in Parker Street just before 11am. Here, due to their unexpected duties, the special 'Manchester's Last Tram' and '1901-1949' banners had to be fitted to the official last car No 1007, in the road, using a cleaning stage. At 11.30am the procession began its 45min journey to Birchfields Road depot — the official end to Manchester's first tramway era. Later that same afternoon the ceremonial cars were driven to Hyde depot, where they were all broken up by 16 March 1949. *Charles F. Klapper*

Right:
In 1946 Sheffield Corporation celebrated 50 years of municipal transport operation by producing prototype double-deck 'Jubilee' car No 501. This used a new form of integral body construction and had a very modern appearance. It was the last car to be built by the Corporation and entered regular service on 12 August 1946. Here, No 501 is seen at Meadowhead, on an LRTL tour of Sheffield held on 22 May 1949. *The late Michael Waller/Peter Waller*

Postwar materials shortages meant that replacement motorbuses, and the fuel to run them on, were not available, so tramways had to carry on. This situation eased by the end of the 1940s, and more and more tramway systems were abandoned in favour of motorbuses. The number of wartime and immediate postwar tramway abandonments per year, were:

1940	3	1945	3
1941	1	1946	3
1942	1	1947	3
1943	0	1948	1
1944	0	1949	8

A few cities displayed their faith and belief in the value of tramways. Leeds, the most acquisitive buyer of second-hand trams — 164 in all — also completed a tramway extension to a housing development at Belle Isle. Planned from 1935, this line had been completed to a temporary terminus at Belle Isle Circus on 22 July 1940. An extension to Middleton Road was opened on 24 February 1946, and two more sections opened — to Belle Isle (Ring Road), on 6 March 1949, and from Belle Isle Top, across country to Middleton (Lingwell

Road), on 28 August 1949 — completing a circular route that was a model of everything a modern tramway should be and could achieve.

Material costs rocketed after the war. Tram rail that had cost £12 per ton in 1939, cost £26 per ton in 1950, and the price of specialist pointwork had increased even more. Another unexpected supply problem arose with electricity after the generating and distribution industries were nationalised on 1 April 1948. Many municipal tramways had been the first major users of locally-generated electricity and were often their local electricity department's largest single customer. Not so to a much larger organisation, who viewed their minority needs with less interest. Also, as the nationalised electricity industry expanded, local generating stations were sidelined and either put on reserve or decommissioned.

New tramcar building declined too, but in the years to 1954 more than 200 new trams would be built by or for six tramway operators. Three of these designs dated from before the war:

■ Edinburgh built 18 'Standard' class cars in 1945-50, to a design from 1934;
■ Aberdeen received 20 Streamliner cars in 1949, to a design from 1940;
■ Glasgow built six 'Coronation' class cars in 1954, using second-hand trucks from Liverpool, to a design from 1937.

Four tramways either built or ordered new designs of tramcars between 1946 and 1954. The first was prototype double-decked car No 501, produced (in Sheffield Corporation's own workshops) in 1946 to celebrate 50 years of municipal transport in the city. Thus the tram was called a 'Jubilee' car, but it, and the nearly identical ones that would follow, would become better known under the maker's name

Top:
Whilst old tramlines were being torn up in Manchester, new ones were being laid down in Leeds. Progress in the work constructing the final section of the Belle Isle-Middleton extension is recorded in this view from May 1949. Track had been laid and, in the distance, some of the overhead strung. *The late Michael Waller/Peter Waller*

Above:
On 21 August 1949, just one week before the Belle Isle-Middleton extension opened, quite a lot of work remained to be done to add a third track at the Middleton terminus at Lingwell Road. Opened on 28 August 1949, the entire Middleton loop scheme had cost Leeds Corporation close on £250,000. Sadly, all of this investment saw just under 10 years' use. The last trams to use the line ran on 28 March 1959. *The late Michael Waller/Peter Waller*

Right:
In need of new tramway rolling stock in 1948, Sheffield Corporation secured a loan sanction of over £200,000 from the Ministry of Transport to order 35 new tramcars based upon the design of 'Jubilee' car No 501. Built by Charles Roberts & Co Ltd, of Horbury, Wakefield, the four-wheeled trams had all-metal bodies with steel frames and aluminium panelling, used air brakes, and had fully upholstered seats on both decks. Christened 'Roberts' cars, No 502, the first to be delivered, entered service on 15 May 1950. It is seen here five days later on a special working. *IAL*

Below:
As London's tramways contracted in the wake of route closures, a number of tram depots became surplus to requirements. Thornton Heath depot stood behind Brigstock House, a building that had served as the headquarters of Croydon Corporation Tramways. The depot had a narrow single-track entrance and was thought to be unsuitable for conversion to a bus garage. Instead it would be demolished and a purpose-built garage erected on the site. Closure came at the end of 1949 and demolition was complete by 3 February 1950. In earlier times, Thornton Heath depot is seen at 11.45am on a rainy day one November — note the wreath on the war memorial tablet on the left. *LTE*

of the production batch: Charles Roberts & Co Ltd, of Horbury, Wakefield. In 1948 Sheffield Corporation secured a loan sanction of over £200,000 from the Ministry of Transport to order 35 tramcars — the first 'Roberts' car, No 502, entering service on 15 May 1950. The four-wheeled trams had all-metal bodies with steel frames and aluminium panelling, used air brakes and provided high levels of passenger comfort, with fully upholstered seats on both decks. Car No 536, the last of the batch, entered service on 11 April 1952.

The other tramways who acquired new tramcars were:

■ Glasgow Corporation — which built 100 'Cunarder' class double-deck tramcars, a design based upon the successful 'Coronation' class of 1937. Their bodies were clad in aluminium and steel, with the main side panels being formed from 20ft long single sheets of birch plywood. The first 'Cunarder', No 1293, entered service on 1 December 1948; the last, No 1392, on 12 February 1952.

■ Blackpool Corporation — which acquired 25 'Coronation' class single-deck tramcars, with bodies produced by Charles Roberts & Co. At 50ft long and 8ft wide, these were the largest trams to run in service in Blackpool. With an all-steel body and four motors, at 19 tons, they were also the heaviest to run there. The first 'Coronation', No 304, entered service on 3 July 1952; the last, No 328, was delivered on 7 January 1954.

■ Leeds Corporation — which obtained two single-deck railcars with bodies by Charles H. Roe Ltd, of Leeds. Their near identical bodies were metal clad, and had a steel floorpan and teak frames, but radically different running gear and control equipment was installed in each, for evaluative purposes. Numbered 601 and 602, the railcars entered service on 1 June 1953. The following year they were joined by No 600, a single-deck tram bought from Sunderland Corporation in 1944 that had been rebuilt in 1945 and 1948, and then reworked to a similar design as Nos 601-2.

Building tramcars in the 1950s was far from easy. Declining orders for trams had forced the established manufacturers to turn to other products, and so interested corporations had difficulties. Glasgow had tried to sub-contract parts of the 'Cunarder' work to outside firms, but faced disinterested firms and rebellion from within their own workforce; and for Charles H. Roe the Leeds railcar bodies would be their only experience of tramcar work.

Tramways were fighting a losing battle against rising material and power costs, declining equipment supplies, freely available motorbuses, and the ever rising popularity of private motoring. Systems closed steadily throughout the 1950s and early 1960s:

1950	3	1957	1
1951	2	1958	1
1952	1	1959	2
1953	1	1960	2
1954	2	1961	1
1955	0	1962	1
1956	3		

Above:
Edinburgh No 169 was one of a final batch of six 'Standard' class cars completed by the Corporation in June 1950. Built to a design from 1934, this used a composite construction with aluminium alloy castings as the body pillars, plywood and aluminium sheets forming the lower body sides and aluminium sheets cladding the upper deck. Passengers saw a patterned ceiling, recessed lighting and enjoyed deep upholstered seating with sponge rubber cushions. These cars entered service two to three months after Edinburgh had abandoned its first tram route and would see just over six years of service there. *Modern Transport/IAL*

Left:
Saturday 4 August 1951 was an important date in UK tramway history, for it was on that day that the last tramcar operated by the Gateshead & District Tramways Co Ltd ran. This was the sole surviving system from the once vast empire controlled by the British Electric Traction Co (BET). Here, Gateshead car No 6 poses beside its replacement. The car was sold on to the Grimsby & Immingham Electric Railway. *IAL*

Trolleybuses, the great alternative to the tramcar in the 1930s, fared little better. Only three new trolleybus systems had opened since 1940:

- Cardiff — 1 March 1942;
- Brighton, Hove & District — 1 January 1945 (although special circumstances were involved and the first vehicles were delivered before the outbreak of World War 2);
- Glasgow — 3 April 1949.

Moreover, by 1949 13 systems had closed. Difficulties with supplies and electricity bedevilled trolleybus operators in the years after World War 2, as they did their tramway colleagues. The wider availability of motorbuses also made an attractive alternative to a vehicle that, although more flexible than a tramcar, was still just as route-bound by its overhead wires. As a result the pace of trolleybus abandonment also quickened — the number of systems closing each year was:

1951	1	1962	1
1952	1	1963	3
1953	2	1964	2
1954	1	1965	1
1955	0	1966	4
1956	2	1967	4
1957	0	1968	3
1958	3	1969	1
1959	2	1970	2
1960	3	1971	1
1961	1	1972	1

Above:
Last tram ceremonies varied considerably, most descended into chaos, and few could match the symmetry of Stockport's. Electric tramway operation began there on 26 August 1901 and was scheduled to end on 25 August 1951 — 50 years exactly. Car No 53 was chosen as Stockport's last tram and is seen full of local dignitaries on the last run from Mersey Square to Reddish and back. The weather, as ever, had a sense of occasion too — it rained. The matching plastic macs and rain hoods sported by the girls on the right were the height of fashion then. *IAL*

Below:
'Operation Tramaway', the programmed abandonment of London's tramways, was divided into eight stages. Number six was the largest before the final withdrawal and took place over the weekend of 5/6 January 1952. Amongst the closures was that of one of the last city termini, at Victoria, seen here with 'E/1' class car No 1672. Through the closures brought about at stage six 115 tramcars were declared surplus to requirements and withdrawn, leaving less than 250 in service on 47 route miles. *IAL*

WE SAY GOODBYE TO LONDON
MUCH TO OUR DELIGHT AND YOUR SORROW WE REALLY CAN'T COME ROUND TOMORROW
LONDON TRANSPORT 20 MORE YEARS WE CAN GO ALAS! ADIEU ACHEERIO R.I.P.

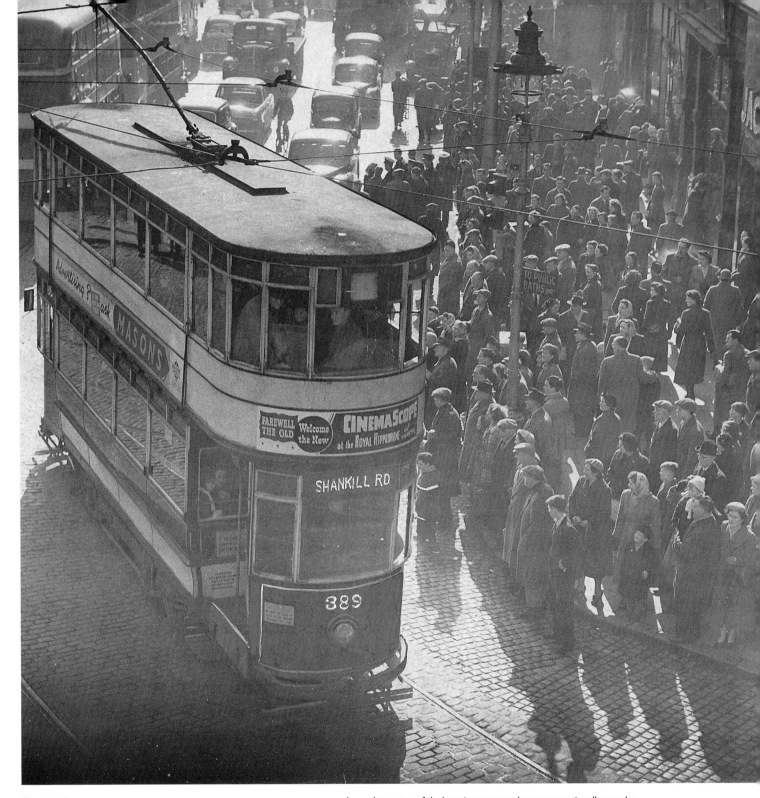

Above:
As Londoners were bidding farewell to their last trams, the bodies for the latest additions to Blackpool's tramcar fleet were taking shape at Charles Roberts & Co's Wakefield works. The 25 'Coronation' class single-deck tramcars had all-steel bodies, with overall dimensions of 50ft long and 8ft wide. This made them the longest, widest and, at 19 tons, the heaviest trams to run in Blackpool. 'Coronation' No 304 was the first to enter service on 3 July 1952; the last, No 328, doing so early in 1954. *IAL*

Right:
The Swansea & Mumbles Railway celebrated its 150th anniversary on 29 June 1954. A replica of the original horse-drawn vehicle used on the line was produced, and a pair of the service cars, led by No 7, were decorated for the occasion and used to convey an invited party to a luncheon at the Guildhall, Swansea. Car No 7 is seen at Rutland Street station, Swansea, on the 150th anniversary day. *IAL*

Right below:
Swansea & Mumbles Railway car No 7 also worked the last service over the line on 5 January 1960. This window sticker was carried on all the trams during the final weeks of operation. No 7 is also the only tangible link left with the line, as one of its cabs has been preserved. An entire tram, No 2, was preserved for 10 years at the Middleton Railway in Leeds, but this was heavily vandalised in 1967 and destroyed by fire in 1970.
Author's Collection

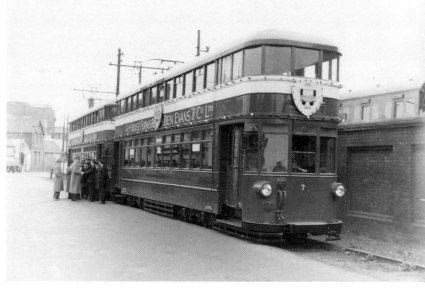

Abandonment of the Mumbles Railway — Tuesday, 5th January, 1960

Normal train service will operate up to and including the following journeys :—

Rutland Street to Southend ———————— 9.55 a.m. Southend to Rutland Street ———————— 10.20 a.m.

The first journeys on the substituted omnibus services will be :—

SERVICE No. 77 : PONTLASSE CROSS—MUMBLES PIER.

Pontlasse Cross to Mumbles Pier ————— dep. 10.5 a.m. Mumbles Pier to Cwmrhydyceirw Cross dep. 10.26 a.m.
Cwmrhydyceirw Cross to Mumbles Pier — " 9.31 a.m.
Guildhall to Mumbles Pier ———————— " 10.0 a.m. Mumbles Pier to Pontlasse Cross ———— " 10.38 a.m.

SERVICE No. 94 : RUTLAND STREET—OYSTERMOUTH SQUARE.

Rutland Street ———————————————— dep. 1.0 p.m. Oystermouth Square ———————————— dep. 1.25 p.m.

FULL DETAILS OF THE TIMETABLES OF THE SUBSTITUTED SERVICES ARE AVAILABLE FROM ANY OF THE COMPANY'S OFFICES OR DIRECT FROM THE HEAD OFFICE.

THE SOUTH WALES TRANSPORT CO., LTD.,
31. RUSSELL STREET, SWANSEA.

"MERCURY." LLANELLY.

The closure of Glasgow's last tram routes on 2 September 1962 left Blackpool as the only town with a working tramway system, but not for long. Exactly eight weeks later, on 28 October, Blackpool Corporation closed its Marton route — the last all-street tramway in the UK. A year later, on 27 October 1963, it also closed the North station branch from Gynn Square, the last street tramway open to the public in the town, leaving just the Promenade and Fleetwood lines. Indeed, as an economy measure, most of Blackpool's tramway closed that day and did not reopen until Good Friday 1964.

To many at the time it must have seemed as though tramways were on the point of extinction in the UK, but the seeds of their preservation and eventual return had been planted 16 years earlier. In 1949 the LRTL had formed a Museum Committee. In 1955 this formed the basis of the Tramway Museum Society (TMS), established as a branch of the LRTL. One of the TMS's main intentions was to preserve tramcars; a task aided by the practice of second-hand tram acquisition practised by a number of tramways in the years after World War 2. A 1903 Southampton tramcar, No 45, was the first to be acquired and, as others were earmarked for preservation, the need to find somewhere to store and then to operate these became increasingly apparent.

Early in 1959 a lease was taken on the site of a former mineral railway serving a stone quarry at Crich in Derbyshire. On 8 May 1959 the first tram, ex-Cardiff water car No 131, was delivered on site, beginning one of the most remarkable preservation stories of the 20th century. The freehold of the site was acquired on 14 January 1961, and in

1963 sufficient track had been laid for horse tram services to begin, courtesy of a hired mare called Bonny. In July 1964 the first electric trams ran at the site and Crich, known as the National Tramway Museum since 1980, has grown to accommodate over 50 trams, with extensive workshop facilities for their repair and restoration, and to provide a home for an impressive library of books, film, papers and photographs, with associated research facilities.

A 2ft gauge electric tramway with origins contemporary to the TMS, ran in Princes Park, Eastbourne until 1969, and now operates at Seaton in Devon. This had its origins in a portable 15in gauge electric tramway built and operated at fêtes by Claude W. Lane. The first car, No 23, was based on the design of two streamlined double-deck trams built for Darwen Corporation in 1936. First run at a fête in Barnet on 2 July 1949, the venture expanded to include a quarter-mile line at Rhyl, commenced in 1952, and the Eastbourne line, opened on 17 September 1953. New trams were built at two-thirds scale, and these incorporated components rescued from trams formerly working in Birmingham, Blackpool, Bournemouth, Glasgow, Grimsby & Immingham, Leeds, Llandudno, London and Sheffield; thereby keeping some of the sounds and feel of these lost tramways alive.

Below:
At the Annual Inspection of Liverpool Corporation's Transport Department, held in December 1954, tramcar No 246, one of 100 'Baby Grand' four-wheeled streamliners built in 1938/39, slips into Edge Lane depot unnoticed. The inspecting party's attention is focused upon the steam cleaning of a Crossley-bodied AEC Regent bus.
Passenger Transport/IAL

Above:
Edinburgh's trams had three months left to run when this view of car No 71 was taken in The Mound, working on route 27 to Granton Road station in August 1956. Eighty-five years of tramway operation ended in the city with a well-ordered and dignified ceremony, involving a procession of 11 cars, held on 16 November 1956. *J. M. Aldridge*

Opposite above:
On 7 November 1957 ex-London 'Feltham' No 511 was the last tram to run through Leeds City Square. Only eight routes then remained from the 29 that had once served the city. This was City Square as work proceeded to remove the tramlines, repeating 'Tramway Occupation' scenes from 60 or so years earlier when they had been laid originally. *Robert F. Mack*

Opposite below:
Liverpool's official last tram was 'Baby Grand' No 293. It was specially painted in reverse livery and photographed with Corporation Transport officials, including W. M. Hall, the General Manager (centre). On 8 September 1957, No 293 re-entered normal service and worked the final week of tramway operation in the city on all the remaining routes: 6, 6a, and 40, and was also the last to run in the tramway closing ceremony held on 14 September 1957. Subsequently No 293 was sold to the Seashore Trolley Museum at Kennebunkport, Maine, USA, where it has the company of other ex-UK tramcars from Blackpool, Glasgow and London. Sadly, visitors to the museum in 1994 reported that No 293 was in a poor condition. *Liverpool Corporation*

Other preserved tramways were developed, including ones at:

- East Anglia Transport Museum at Carlton Colville, near Lowestoft;
- North East Open Air Museum at Beamish;
- Black Country Museum at Dudley.

The last-named is the only working 3ft 6in gauge tramway in the UK. New tramcar building also resumed briefly after 30 years, when Blackpool Corporation ordered the body for the first of eight 'Centenary' cars from East Lancashire Coachbuilders of Blackburn in 1984. A marriage of bus body panels, the first completed car, No 641, entered service in the town on 4 July 1984. A total of eight were built.

The 1980s saw a much belated recognition by policy and decision makers that electrically-operated light rail vehicles could play an important role in the mass movement of people, especially within conurbations. A number of schemes were promoted, but the first to be built and to operate were the Manchester Metrolink, which opened on 6 April 1992, and the Sheffield Supertram which opened to the public on 21 March 1994. By 27 February 1995, five services were being operated on three routes, with more to follow. Just under two months later UK tramway history turned full circle when, on 14 April 1995, the first 400yd section of a street-running tourist tramway opened in Birkenhead, where 135 years earlier, our story began.

This book records aspects of the UK's first tramway era — the second one has just begun.

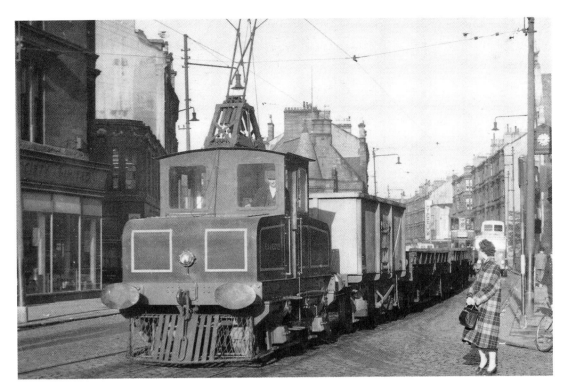

Opposite:
The introduction of trolleybus route 108 in Glasgow on 15 November 1958 was the last tram-to-trolleybus conversion in the UK. Part of the route also used Govan Road, seen here in 1959 with BUT trolleybus No TB95 working wrong wire as road resurfacing work continues. Electric locomotives from the Fairfield Shipbuilding & Engineering Co still continued to use the former tramlines, which remained in place for a while. *Ian Maclean*

Top:
In Glasgow's Govan Road trams had to share their tracks with the electric locomotives of the Fairfield Shipbuilding & Engineering Co. The system's track gauge was 4ft 7³/₄in, ³/₄in narrower than standard gauge, to allow ordinary railway wagons to run with their flanges in the grooves. Trams last ran in Govan Road on 14 November 1958, but the overhead remained, adapted for the replacement trolleybus services and for use by Fairfield's locomotives. *W. F. Cameron*

Above:
The Grimsby & Immingham Electric Railway was built by the Great Central Railway to link the town of Grimsby with their new dock at Immingham. It opened on 15 May 1912 and was heavily used. Passing in turn to the LNER and British Railways, the original rolling stock was supplemented by the purchase of 21 trams from Gateshead and Newcastle in 1948-1951. Use of the line was weakened when a street running section at the Grimsby end was closed on 1 July 1956. By 1960 most of the line's passengers had been siphoned away by the improvement of a competing road and a rival bus service that used it. Closure loomed and came on 1 July 1961. In happier times, car No 15, of 1915, waits at Grimsby Corporation Bridge station on 19 May 1954. *R. E. Vincent*

Opposite:
Tragedy marred the final years of Glasgow's tramways. On 28 January 1959 three people were killed when a tram struck a lorry in Shettleston Road and burst into flames. Fire also struck Dalmarnock depot on 22 March 1961, destroying 50 trams. Short of anywhere else to store and operate the cars from, the depot remained in use but roofless. This was how it looked in September 1961, with 'Coronation' No 1242 nearest to the camera. The last day of regular tramway operation in Glasgow was 1 September 1962. A ceremonial procession of historic trams ran on 4 September, and events concluded with the running of special services on 6 September. *D. F. Parker*

Right:
The National Tramway Museum at Crich has now been in operation for more than 30 years — longer, in many instances, than the tramway systems that are represented by trams in the collection. Constructed in part along the alignment of a mineral railway that once served the limestone quarry, the Museum site now houses an impressive array of buildings, including the facade of the Derby Assembly Rooms and the recently completed exhibition hall. Blackpool 'Standard' No 40 is pictured in June 1975; this scene has in recent years been transformed by the construction of the Bowes Lyon bridge in the background.
The late Michael H. Waller/Peter Waller

Right:
Glasgow's closure left Blackpool as the only town in the UK with a tramway system, but a series of route closures would reduce this to just the Promenade and Fleetwood routes in little over a year. Blackpool closed its tram routes at the ends of its holiday seasons, which were extended by the town's famous illuminations. On 29 October 1961 trams were withdrawn on the routes to Cabin and Bispham from Squires Gate, and from South Pier to Marton. Here, on a journey to Cabin, a 'Balloon' double-decker is followed along Lytham Road by a 'Pantograph' car on 19 May 1954. *Robert F. Mack*

Below:
Blackpool's next round of route closures occurred on 28 October 1962 and saw trams withdrawn from the Royal Oak and Talbot Square routes to Marton. Eleven years earlier, on 15 August 1951, an unidentified Marton 'Vambac' car (named after the Variable Automatic Multinotch Braking and Acceleration Control equipment fitted to these 12 cars) is seen loading in Talbot Square. *IAL*

Above:
The final round of Blackpool route closures came on 27 October 1963 with the withdrawal of the North station-Cabin/Fleetwood services. Thus constricted to the Starr Gate-Fleetwood service, Blackpool's tramway is none the less a national treasure, capable, on occasions, of producing a spectacular ride. Here, one day in April 1969, Brush-built car No 631 (ex-No 294) produces a spark from its wheels during one of Blackpool's celebrated storms. *IAL*

Right:
Together with the Manchester Metrolink scheme, Sheffield's growing Supertram system has ushered in the second tramway era in the UK, and it is the first to be mainly street-based. The first line, to Meadowhall, opened on 21 March 1994. Car No 1002 was the first to be delivered from its makers in Düsseldorf, arriving at Immingham Docks — possibly the first tram to do so since the Grimsby & Immingham Electric Railway closed in July 1961! With a top speed of 50mph, each car carries 250 passengers, 88 of whom can be seated. *South Yorkshire Supertram Ltd/Author's Collection*

Right:
The UK's first purpose-built street-running tourist tramway also began to operate in 1995. Linking the Woodside Ferry terminus with Pacific Road in Birkenhead, this 400yd tramway runs close to the route worked by G. F. Train's first UK tramway in 1860. Opened on 14 April 1995, the line is operated by Blackpool Transport Services and worked by two four-wheel double-deck trams, Nos 69 and 70, built by Hong Kong Tramways Ltd. Illustrated is car No 70 heading along Shore Road on 29 May 1995. *Author*

TRAMWAY ARCHAEOLOGY

As trams return to UK streets there are still plenty of artefacts and reminders to be found from the nation's first era of tramway development. Most of the examples in this section come from the author's native Black Country, where trams last ran in the early 1930s. That so many of these items can still be found over 60 years after they were last needed by a tramway shows the great potential for similar discoveries to be made in other areas. Good hunting!

TRACK

During World War 2 a number of local authorities who had redundant tram tracks in their streets made great play of digging these up and donating them as scrap for the war effort. Together with railings from around public buildings, this was a ready way for councils both to do their bit and to set an example for others to follow. Despite this drive, some track escaped and lies dormant beneath layers of tarmac waiting to be discovered. So it is always worth taking a look if there are ever any major roadworks where trams once ran.

Left:
The Fish, Amblecote, 6 March 1994: that portion of the Kinver Light Railway's track between its start, by The Fish Inn at Amblecote, and The Ridge in Wollaston, had long been rumoured to remain in place beneath the road surface. A junction realignment at Amblecote early in 1994 required the stripping away of decades of tarmac and, on 5 March 1994, revealed the substance beneath the rumours. Photographed the following morning, this view shows the results of half-an-hour's effort on the author's part, spent kicking and scuffing away surface clutter to reveal the rails and their associated setts. The Fish Inn can be seen at right, and beyond is the KLR's former depot. *Author*

Above:
Hyde Road, Manchester, 29 August 1991: as the UK's first new tramlines for decades were being laid, simultaneously, a mile or so away in the city centre, roadworks revealed buried survivors from the Manchester's first tramway system. These tracks were last used by trams in service on 17 May 1948. *Author*

OVERHEAD EQUIPMENT

When tramway routes or systems were abandoned, overhead wires were removed very quickly, unless they were shared by trolleybuses. Overlooked tramway overhead is therefore impossible to find, but a lot of the equipment associated with supporting and supplying it can still be identified. Some local authorities adapted traction poles to serve as lamp standards, and these can still be recognised by the jaunty angle at which they lean back once freed from the weight and tension of their wires. In narrow streets, where there was no room for traction poles, the overhead was strung directly between facing buildings and attached to these by means of a mounting plate called a 'rosette', some of which remain in place. Overhead was divided into half-mile sections, each of which could be isolated in the case of damage or an accident. At each of these section breaks there was a gang of switches, held within a slender metal casing called, variously, a 'switch pillar', 'isolator hatch' or 'junction box'. Often adorned with the tramway operator's initials, crest or symbol, these pillars survive in some locations, partly because they are so difficult to remove.

Above:
Cotteridge Depot, Birmingham, 6 July 1985: five months before its closure was announced; thin layers of tarmac have worn away to reveal the single entrance track to the former tram depot. Opened on 23 June 1904, Cotteridge was a working tram depot for 48 years, closing with services along the Pershore Road on 4 July 1952. Converted to use as a bus garage, services last worked from there on 25 October 1986. A number of bus garages that were built as tram depots have retained their tramlines, removing them being too disruptive to the running of the garage. *Author*

Right:
Stewpony Inn, Kinver, 8 May 1991: although famed for having wooden traction poles along its roadside and cross-country sections, the only traction pole to survive from the Kinver Light Railway's overhead is a metal one. It can be seen standing just behind the Parish Council's notice board, and its position gives one of the few clues to the tramway's alignment through what is now a very busy and much altered road junction. The last service tram ran on the KLR on 8 February 1930. *Author*

Above:
High Lodge Farm, Norton, 27 March 1994: the Kinver Light Railway had two depots, and both survive. The first to be built was in Hyde Meadow in Kinver; it opened in July 1901. For many years it was believed that this had been demolished because its inspection pits and a few rails could be found, with some difficulty, amongst the undergrowth. This was not the case. The depot had in fact been moved to a farm a few miles away and re-erected to serve as a cattle shed. Here it stands, minus two of its original four pairs of doors, and plus some lean-tos, but otherwise substantially as it was built to accommodate trams 93 years ago. *Author*

Left:
Foster Street, Stourbridge, 8 May 1991: easily confused with a building reinforcing plate; the device bolted to the upper storey of the West Bromwich Building Society is in fact a tramway overhead rosette. Foster Street was the point where the tramway to Lye branched off the High Street line in Stourbridge, but it was too narrow to allow traction poles to be used to support the overhead. Rosettes were mounted on to the buildings instead, and this is the last one to survive *in situ*, others having been recovered for preservation. The Lye route opened on 1 November 1902 and closed on 5 February 1927. *Author*

Opposite:
Heaton Park Tramway, Manchester, 31 May 1984: although preserved, this switch pillar, from the Oldham, Ashton & Hyde Electric Tramway Ltd, exemplifies all the features of these pieces of overhead equipment. The 'Magnet & Wheel' device signifies that the company was a subsidiary of the British Electric Traction Co, whose symbol this was, and the initials beneath record that the pillar was made by the British Thomson-Houston Co Ltd. Inserting a key into the hole at right, opened the front hatch to give access to the switches inside. Made from cast-iron, the pillar extends beneath the ground for a distance equivalent to about half its height. *Author*

Left:
Stourton, 5 May 1991: there are two legacies of the Kinver Light Railway to be seen in this view of a bend in the Bridgnorth Road as it heads towards The Stewpony. On the left is a wide grass verge that was formerly the KLR's trackbed. The wide portion, with the direction sign on it, was a passing place, where two loops branched out from the main single line. On the right is a footpath that parallels the trackbed all the way to The Stewpony. This was built by the tramway company at the insistence of the Parish Council, which was concerned that people might otherwise be tempted to walk along the tramway, in peril of their own safety. The KLR last ran on 8 February 1930. *Author*

Below:
The Fish, Amblecote, 8 May 1991: the Kinver Light Railway's second depot was at its Amblecote terminus, opposite The Fish Inn. Here the company built a battery booster sub-station in 1902. When it needed extra depot capacity a four-road depot was also built there, opening in October 1905. Above, left to right, can be seen a 1908 extension to the battery booster station, the four-road depot of 1905, and a two road extension to this, also added in 1908. Closed as a working depot on 12 May 1926, Amblecote was used to store trams until the KLR closed on 8 February 1930 and since then it has been a potato warehouse and, latterly, a laser games centre. Despite these changes in use and ownership, the tracks still remain inside the 1905 shed. *Author*

Above:
Kingsway Subway, south of Holborn station, 16 August 1992: parties are occasionally led down the subway, and being a part of one of these allowed this shot to be taken. Lugging a camera, flash and tripod, and straying a little beyond the proscribed limit, produced this view of encroaching darkness as the subway heads south towards Aldwych. Both conduit slots are clearly visible, as is a little-used crossover running left to right. The recesses were for maintenance workers to tuck themselves into when trams passed. Above is the steel girder roof, installed when the subway was enlarged in 1929/30. *Author*

Below:
Perry Park Road, Old Hill, 5 May 1991: to complete the Dudley, Stourbridge & District Electric Traction Co Ltd's (DS&DET) system the company wanted to build a line linking Old Hill to Blackheath, which stood 100ft above. The existing road between the towns was too steep, and so the DS&DET decided to build their own. Known locally as 'The Tump', Perry Park Road came into use with the tramway on 29 November 1904. Although the last trams to use the road ran on 30 June 1927, it survives, little altered, as an excellent illustration of the curves and gradients that electric trams could take in their stride. This is the first sharp bend on the ascent of Perry Park Road. *Author*

DEPOTS

Tram depots were very adaptable buildings. Usually well built, and often with large covered floor areas, mostly unencumbered by supporting stanchions, they were easily converted to other uses. Some became bus garages, but others found a variety of second and third careers as garages, pubs, restaurants, theatres and warehouses, amongst others.

ROADS

Constructing tramways sometimes required the alteration of existing roads or the formation of new ones to accommodate tramcar operation and its tolerances for curves and gradients. Many decades after trams ceased to run, some of these specially altered or formed roads remain, often remarkably little changed.

A TRAMWAY MONUMENT

If nominations were ever sought for the premier monument to tramways in the UK, then the Kingsway Subway in London would come very high, if not top, of the list. Following its closure on 5 April 1952 it was used for 10 years to store buses and machine parts, before work began to convert its southern part into a road underpass beneath The Strand, which opened on 21 January 1964. The northern part housed temporary buildings that acted as the control room for London's flood control, but was otherwise unaltered. With the flood control centre now closed, the subway's future is again uncertain. Restoration as a working tramway subway?